WHAT MAKES A HERO?

What Makes a Hero?
The Death-Defying Ministry of Jesus

What Makes a Hero?
978-1-5018-4792-9
978-1-5018-4793-6 eBook

What Makes a Hero? DVD
978-1-5018-4796-7

What Makes a Hero? Leader Guide
978-1-5018-4794-3
978-1-5018-4795-0 eBook

What Makes a Hero? Youth Study Book
978-1-5018-4803-2
978-1-5018-4804-9 eBook

What Makes a Hero? Children's Leader Guide
978-1-5018-4791-2

What Makes a Hero? Worship Resources
978-1-5018-4805-6 Flash Drive
978-1-5018-4806-3 Download

Also by Matt Rawle

The Faith of a Mockingbird
Hollywood Jesus
The Salvation of Doctor Who
The Redemption of Scrooge

MATT RAWLE

WHAT MAKES A
HERO?
THE DEATH-DEFYING
MINISTRY OF JESUS

Abingdon Press / Nashville

What Makes a Hero?
The Death-Defying Ministry of Jesus

This book is printed on elemental chlorine-free paper.
Library of Congress Cataloging-in-Publication data has been requested.

978-1-5018-4792-9

17 18 19 20 21 22 23 24 25 26 — 10 9 8 7 6 5 4 3 2 1
MANUFACTURED IN THE UNITED STATES OF AMERICA

To Rev. James Philip Woodland.
He was a hero to many, and a saint to all.

CONTENTS

INTRODUCTION

What names come to mind when you hear the word *hero*? Whom would you imitate if you were called upon to be a hero? Do you imagine a character from the pages of a comic book, or someone who taught you important life lessons?

Though the names and faces might be different, most of us share a similar picture of who is a hero. Our fictional and real-life heroes all know separation, trial, and in one way or another, we all share these same experiences.

Our heroes represent the stories we wish we could tell about ourselves. Whether they don capes in comic books, selflessly run into burning buildings to save lives, break athletic records, or march in the streets to end injustice, heroes are set apart into different categories than the rest of us. They offer us stories of transformation and lessons in how to understand the world. They offer us examples of who we wish we could be.

We find heroes in comic books, in history, in our own lives. There are heroes in the Bible. Jesus was a hero. But what makes a hero?

In his groundbreaking book *The Hero with a Thousand Faces*, American mythologist Joseph Campbell analyzed myths from cultures around the world and found some fascinating patterns.[1] Virtually all cultures have hero stories that have elements in common:

- Ordinary world
- Call to adventure
- Crossing the threshold
- Challenges and temptations
- Death and resurrection
- Return home with the reward

This pattern, the hero's journey, appears over and over again in our myths and stories.[2] Our superhero narratives nearly always follow this progression, and even the story of Jesus contains elements of the hero's journey. We will explore it further in this book, using examples ranging from pop culture to our daily lives. We'll be discussing good and evil, right and wrong. We'll consider the hero's role in the struggles between us and them, haves and have-nots, old and new, and life and death. Through it all, we will look at our greatest hero, Jesus—how he took the world's view of courage, turned it on its head, and forever redefined what a hero is.

THE POP IN CULTURE

What comes to mind when you hear someone refer to pop culture? Do you think of movies and colorful characters, or a childhood spent poring over comic book stories? These days, we often associate pop culture with television and the characters and personalities we find there. Pop culture is definitely the home for many of our heroes, both fictional superheroes and the real-life role models we look up to. Many of the stories we want to tell about ourselves are rooted in what we find in our pop culture accounts.

Regardless if you think an example of pop culture is the latest *Superman* comic or something more edgy like *The Walking Dead*, there's no denying that the popular music, books, television, movies, and media have much to say about the world in which we live. The word *culture* is used often by many different people in many different ways, but in its simplest form, *culture* is simply an expression of how a community understands itself. God, our Creator, supplies us with the raw ingredients of humanity—talents, time, creativity, desires, ingenuity—and culture is whatever we cook up. Stories, songs, recipes, traditions, art, and language are all displays of how we interpret the world and our place in it.

So what role does God play in our culture—in our day-to-day lives and in the work of our hands, which produces music and art and crafts and literature and plays and movies and technology? Throughout history, people have debated this issue and adamantly drawn a dividing line between that which should be considered *sacred* (that which is explicitly religious in nature) and that which should be considered *secular* (that is, everything else). At first

11

glance, these may be seemingly easy judgments to make, but when we stop to examine what God has to say about this division, we might be surprised at what we find.

Scripture says that all things were made through Christ (John 1:3), and through Christ all things were reconciled to God (Colossians 1:20). In other words, everything and everyone in our world contains a spark of the divine—everything is sacred, and whether or not we choose to live in that truth depends on our perspective. For example, think of sunlight as a holy (sacred) gift from God. God offers us sunlight so we can see the world around us. We can celebrate the sacred by creating things that enhance the light in our homes, such as larger windows or skylights, or we can hang heavy drapes and close the shutters in order to diminish the sacred and shut out the light. Our sacred work is letting in as much light as possible, and those things that keep the light out need to be rejected or transformed. Through Jesus, God put on flesh and walked among us in our world in order to re-narrate what it means to be a child of God.

God assumed culture and transformed it. So now all is sacred, and in everything we are to see and proclaim his glory. I truly believe we are called not to reject the culture we live in, but to re-narrate its meaning—to tell God's story in the midst of it. Jesus didn't reject the cross (the sin of our world); rather, Jesus accepted it and transformed it from a death instrument into a symbol of life and reconciliation.

Sometimes it's easy to see God in the midst of culture—in the stories of Scripture and in reverent hymns and worshipful icons. Stories of heroes and superheroes often preach the gospel pretty clearly, I think. But other times the divine is more veiled—hidden in a novel, concealed in classic rock, obscured by an impressionist's palate. That is why we created this Pop in Culture series, a collection of studies about faith and popular culture. Each study uses a feature of pop culture—in this case, heroes and superheroes—as a way to examine questions and issues of the Christian faith. Our hope and prayer is that the studies will open our eyes to the spiritual truths that exist all around us in books, movies, music, and television.

As we walk with Christ, we discover the divine all around us, and in turn, the world invites us into a deeper picture of its Creator. Through this lens of God's redemption story, we are invited to look at culture in a new and inviting way. We are invited to dive into the realms of literature, art, and entertainment to explore and discover how God is working in and through us and in the world around us to tell God's great story of redemption. With God, we can tell our own heroic stories of triumph and heroism.

Chapter 1

GOOD, EVIL, AND GOD

After a young Bruce Wayne witnessed the murder of his parents one night in a dark alley, the force behind Batman was born. Out of a desire to fight the kinds of criminals that changed his life that night, Bruce Wayne became a force of good dressed as a bat and armed with finely tuned physical and intellectual skills. He vowed never to use deadly force. From his inception in 1939, Batman has overcome adversity to become a pop-culture hero who continues to fight crime and inspire viewers to this day. In his relentless fight against the evil forces of the world, Batman has become a hero to millions of readers and viewers throughout the world.

Heroes lie at the center of the good-versus-evil stories we tell. Whether we are wide-eyed in front of the latest Batman movie, glued to Saturday-morning action cartoons, or puzzling through the vivid images in the Book of Revelation, we are drawn to the struggle between good and evil. When the Empire does strike back in the classic Star Wars film, we just know that the heroic Jedi will return and there will be a happy ending. Why does everything feel right when the cowboy in the white hat foils the plot of the hunched, mustached villain? How do we know that good will always win in the end? Could it be that we want the forces of good to win because we think that good is on our side?

The struggle between good and evil is so fundamental to understanding the world around us that across cultures we share a common story told in different ways. The heroes of our stories are characters who represent all of us. They are men and women who help us understand what is good, and they fight for what's right. We see ourselves in the hero stories we tell, which might be why our heroes never have it too easy. If Superman never sweats, the story isn't interesting, and we no longer identify with it. Our heroes are human. They struggle, fight, and persevere, but no matter the odds, they are victorious in the end.

Even though we like to see ourselves in our heroes' stories, our heroes are very much *not* like us. They are stronger than our muscles can manage and wiser than our feeble minds can comprehend. They move faster than our own clumsy bodies. They are not confined to past, present, and future. The hero is a picture of who we are and what we can never be, and this is why we need them.

A NEW KIND OF HERO

Be imitators of God, as beloved children, and
live in love as Christ loved us and gave himself up
for us.

Ephesians 5:1-2

We look up to our heroes as role models, and we find in them great sources of inspiration. There is a natural desire to imitate the people we most admire. When there was a controversy in the church in Ephesus, Paul urged the congregation, "Be imitators of God, as beloved children, and live in love as Christ loved us and gave himself up for us" (Ephesians 5:1-2). Paul urges the congregation to imitate God's works by imitating what Jesus has done. In this way, Jesus takes on the role of a hero for us, and we seek to imitate his behavior because he is the supreme example of goodness and love.

Imitation is one of the first ways we learn about the world. I witnessed this in action one evening while I was giving my daughter a bath. "What does a duck say? Quack, quack!" I asked, as I paraded a yellow rubber ducky around the waves of lukewarm bathwater. I asked again, but before I could finish the question, she looked up at me and said, "Quack, quack!" I stopped. My face lit up with excitement. I asked again, "What does a duck say?" She answered, "Quack, quack!"

My daughter wasn't actually saying that a duck quacks; rather, she was mimicking my words in the game we had been playing for a couple of weeks. It's like a golfer watching videos of other golfers' swings, vocalists listening to famous opera singers, a student-teacher observing a third-grade classroom, or a child watching his dad clean a fish. We learn who we want to be by imitating those we already look up to. Imitation helps us discover the world around us, and our place within it.

At some point, we move away from imitation, and we begin to tell our own stories. We carefully step away from what is familiar, and we launch ourselves into the dangerous unknown, just like our beloved heroes before us. Both Luke Skywalker and Superman had to leave their home planets and strike out into an unknown world.

Do you remember a time when you took those first few steps away from what you knew? Maybe it was when you began to drive, and you visited a side of town you didn't know existed. Maybe you took a job offer and moved halfway across the country. Maybe it was when the doctor announced, "It's a girl!" and you quickly realized that your world was about to be turned upside down.

Batman's story began with a separation, when Bruce Wayne lost his parents. Jesus' ministry also started with a separation, but of a very different kind. In his letter to the Philippians, Paul writes:

> *Christ Jesus,*
> *who, though he was in the form of God,*
>   *did not regard equality with God*
>   *as something to be exploited,*
> *but emptied himself,*
>   *taking the form of a slave,*
>   *being born in human likeness.*
> *And being found in human form,*
>   *he humbled himself*

and became obedient to the point of death—
even death on a cross.

Philippians 2:5-8

Christ "emptied himself," to take on the flesh and blood of humanity in its fullness. He left behind all that was familiar for the sake of humanity. For example, before washing the feet of his disciples, Jesus "got up from the table, took off his outer robe, and tied a towel around himself" (John 13:4). He shed his outer robe in order to join the disciples and become a servant to them. This wasn't a loss so much as a way that Jesus welcomed the disciples, and us, into God's divine story. In other words, what we see as separation in our heroes' tales is understood as hospitality and sacrifice in the Gospel stories.

Once heroes muster the courage to separate themselves from the familiar, they often find themselves in the midst of trials that must be overcome for the story to continue. Not long after Princess Moana sailed away from Motunui in the Disney film *Moana*, she came face to face with the evil Kakamora. In order to find redemption, the Roman god Hercules had to complete twelve labors for King Eurystheus. In the Bible, David walked out onto the battlefield with a sling and a rock to face the towering Goliath, who mocked him on the other side. No matter the odds, it seems our heroes overcome whatever gets in their way.

Our heroes succeed through feats of strength, unparalleled cleverness, or the sheer unwillingness to give up. Jesus himself faced trials during his ministry: the temptation in the wilderness, frustration with the disciples who never seemed to understand, betrayal by Judas, denial by Peter, and ultimately death by crucifixion. Unlike other heroes, though, Jesus did not turn to strength, cleverness, or stubbornness in order to overcome his trials. He did not remove himself from the cross through divine strength. He did not outsmart Pontius Pilate. Instead, Jesus submitted to the agony of being nailed to the cross, he breathed his last, and he was buried in a garden tomb. But there was still a victory. Jesus' victory over death was not about power, or might, or God being stronger than the grave; rather, Jesus revealed God's desire that life would always have the final and everlasting word.

Jesus' story is both familiar and completely separate from us. His life, suffering, death, and resurrection mirror our own hero stories in many ways, but Jesus' story is much different. Jesus is the Messiah. It's not that Jesus is better, or stronger, or quicker, or wittier than the rest of us. Jesus *is* us, and at the same time he is altogether different. When we look to Jesus' story we find a common thread, but we also find that the thread is woven into a subversive, upside-down revelation of God's kingdom. Jesus is a new kind of hero.

Who are some of your heroes? What makes them heroic?

How can you be a hero in someone's life?

In what ways are you imitating Jesus' life?

SUPERHEROES

Batman[1]

Comic

Publisher: DC Comics
Created by: Bill Finger and Bob Kane
First appeared in: *Detective Comics* #27, March 1939

Character

Alter ego: Bruce Wayne
Species: Human
Hometown: Gotham City
Currently resides in: Gotham City
Teams: The Bat Family; Justice League

Powers

Genius-level intellect
Peak physical and mental conditioning
Extremely skilled martial artist and fighter
Detective skills
A wide array of highly advanced technological equipment
and weapons, such as

- The Batmobile
- An armored Batsuit
- The Bat-signal, which is used to call Batman when his help is needed

Notable enemies

The Joker
The Penguin
Two-Face
The Riddler

SUPERHEROES

Interesting fact

In most representations of the character, Batman refuses to use guns to fight crime due to a gun being the weapon that killed his parents. Bruce has had an extreme dislike of guns ever since.

Origin

One night when Bruce Wayne was a young boy, he went to the theater with his parents. In a dark alley, a thief kills both parents in front of Bruce. Deeply affected by the murder and loss, Bruce begins to train himself both mentally and physically to be able to fight criminals. He adopts the symbol of a bat because he was very afraid of bats as a child, and he wants to strike that fear into the criminals he pursues. Once Batman is born, Bruce continues to run his father's company during the day and fight crime by night.

Heroic moment

After a long search, Batman finally corners the evil and dangerous Joker in an abandoned building. Just as he is about to catch him, he hears the cry of a little girl trapped in the building. Batman chooses to save the girl even though it means letting the Joker get away.[2]

DISCERNING THE GOOD

A good tree cannot bear bad fruit, nor can a
bad tree bear good fruit.

Matthew 7:18

One of the things that sets heroes apart from the rest of us is their solid understanding of good versus evil. Sometimes it's easy to tell the difference. We know instinctively that Superman is the good guy and Lex Luthor is the bad guy, but it's not always that simple. Maybe goodness is much more subjective than we are comfortable admitting. We see this in the story of King David, who early in his reign was seen as "like the angel of God, discerning good and evil" (2 Samuel 14:17). Near the end of his life, his vision became cloudy and dim, and when his son Solomon usurped the throne, David didn't even realize it (1 Kings 1:18). If we can imagine that King David wrestled with understanding goodness, then what hope is there for us?

Sometimes when we think about what is good, we think about the feeling something produces or how well something worked. Goodness, however, goes beyond a nice feeling or something pleasant. I know a good buffalo wing sauce when I taste one, but I would be hard-pressed to say something moral about it. Medicine can offer healing, lower a fever, and keep our minds alert, but ask any toddler how good it is to swallow an antibiotic!

Goodness also contains more than just how effective something is, like a good plan or a good sermon. Some Sundays when I've preached a good sermon, people enjoy the message but nothing good comes from it. Other Sundays when I didn't feel confident about my preaching, a new ministry is born and people ask to join our church.

Often, we judge goodness according to the result it produces. It's like when Jesus warned against following false prophets by saying, "A good tree cannot bear bad fruit, nor can a bad tree bear good fruit" (Matthew 7:18). It's true that we will know goodness according to its fruit, but it's not the fruit that makes the tree good. The work we do doesn't make us good or bad, and neither do those works earn or lose us salvation. Instead, the work we produce is a sign of our connection with God.

God is the source of good. Instead of thinking about goodness as what is pleasant or effective, we must understand that good is simply our word for God's activity in the world. But how can we tell which activities are of God and which are not? We could say that the good, the bad, and the ugly all come from God; but this doesn't sound like the gospel. Perspective matters. I've heard it said that God doesn't give you more than you can handle, but this suggests that it is God who is the one giving you trouble. This doesn't sound like the Gospel either.

Not everything we experience is from God. Trials, stumbling blocks, despair, and violence are not God's way of testing our faith. As Jesus says, "Every plant that my heavenly Father has not planted will be uprooted" (Matthew 15:13). There are accidents, and tragedies, and atrocities that just happen, and those are not planted by God. Sometimes the most loving word we can hear or offer is difficult. Intervening when a loved one is struggling with addiction, refusing to stay in an abusive relationship, and speaking truth to power are far from pleasant endeavors, but they are good.

When do we finally understand something to be good or evil? Heroes seem to have a bent toward the big picture. In an old

Chinese tale about good luck and bad luck, a farmer went out and found that his horse had run away and his neighbor said, "What bad luck." The farmer replied, "Good luck, bad luck, who knows?" The next day the horse came back with three other horses and his neighbor replied, "What good luck!" The farmer said, "Good luck, bad luck, who knows?" The next day the horses trampled the man's garden, destroying his crop. His neighbor said, "What bad luck." The farmer replied, "Good luck, bad luck, who knows?" The next season his garden produced twice as many vegetables because the soil had been turned, and his neighbor said. . . . Things change with time and circumstance, and sometimes it's only by looking at the big picture that we can discern the good.

Rarely do you see heroes struggle to understand the difference between good and evil. They seem to know and to move into action. The rest of us aren't so gifted. Life can seem grayer than we are comfortable admitting. Thankfully, we don't have to spend much time deciding. When we do works of justice, mercy, and humility, we will see God, the source of goodness, working through all that we do.

Have you experienced something unpleasant that ended up being a good thing?

Have you experienced something you thought was great that resulted in something not so great?

Some things we experience are not from God. So, where are they from? Does it matter?

EVIL AND NOTHINGNESS

I cry to you and you do not answer me;
I stand, and you merely look at me.
                                        Job 30:20

I don't spend too much time talking about evil because there is sometimes a temptation to present evil as more interesting than good. It's like preaching on Judas during Holy Week, or on the devil during Lent. These might make colorful sermons, but they would miss the point. Just as goodness goes beyond how something feels or how effective something is, evil is not just what feels terrible or what fails.

Evil is nothingness. Much as *good* is our word for what God does, *evil* represents a void. Evil is nothing in the sense that it cannot stand on its own. Heroes reveal to us what it is we are striving for. Heroes can almost immediately tell the difference between good and evil because they are repelled by evil's nothingness.

The figure of the devil has its roots in the character named Satan, who is mentioned in the books of Job and Zechariah. The devil is evil personified, which places our understanding of the devil in a bit of a paradox. Evil is a shadow that cannot stand on its own. A shadow by itself is nothing but the absence of light. Theologically speaking, evil is made manifest when someone or something stands between us and the light of God shining through Christ. One way to look at evil is by thinking about the number -2. It is impossible to have -2 of something. I can't hold it in my hand. I can't put it in a box because -2 doesn't exist; at least, it only exists as an absence. You can have 2 fewer than something, but you can never have -2 in and of itself. The devil, being a manifestation of nothingness, places him in a paradox. The devil is the manifestation of nothingness, which drives him mad because he cannot exist within the grace of God. The devil is a shadow. Shadows are real, but they are only seen when we block the light. So, when we surround ourselves with the light of the resurrection, in essence, the devil does not exist.

As we explore good and evil, it's helpful to study loss and the emptiness it brings. One of the most profound stories about loss comes in the Book of Job. The saga begins almost like a superhero origin story: "There was once a man in the land of Uz whose name was Job. That man was blameless and upright, one who feared God and turned away from evil" (Job 1:1). Right from the beginning, the author frames the story with a stark contrast: you can either be upright or evil.

One day, the heavenly council gathers together for a staff meeting. God boasts about how blameless and upright Job is. Satan, playing the appropriate role of devil's advocate, suggests that if Job weren't so blessed in his life, he could end up cursing God. The Lord accepts Satan's challenge, and allows Satan to take control of all that Job loves with one condition: he cannot hurt Job himself in any way. In this story, evil is less about what happens to us and more about how we respond to what happens. This is our hero's obstacle to face, and as the story unfolds, Job copes with the misfortune and tragedy that befall him.

As his fortunes change and he begins to lose his possessions and the people he loves, Job succumbs to what sounds a lot like depression:

> *"And now my soul is poured out within me;*
> *days of affliction have taken hold of me.*

The night racks my bones,
*   and the pain that gnaws me takes no rest. . . .*
I cry to you and you do not answer me;
*   I stand, and you merely look at me.*
You have turned cruel to me;
*   with the might of your hand you persecute*
*   me. . . .*
I go about in sunless gloom."

Job 30:16-17, 20-21, 28a

In this circumstance, Job is heroic in his honesty and his suffering. He is in despair, but he is also angry at God. He says, "As God lives, who has taken away my right, / and the Almighty, who has made my soul bitter" (Job 27:2). But even through the bitterness of his soul, Job remains in conversation with God. He opens the way for all of us to experience a range of emotions with God, and this is the culmination of his hero's journey, the saving message he delivers through his story to help those who will read it for generations.

Does this mean that Satan won the great divine wager? Did Job turn from his upright ways? The text isn't clear. What the text *does* make clear is that God answers Job "out of the whirlwind" and says, in effect, "Hang on! I'm about to blow your mind." God takes him on a tour of the universe, showing Job the most beautiful things that God can muster. In other words, God answers Job's depression with beauty itself.

Evil is nothing in the sense that it cannot stand on its own. It's like a shadow. When God brought forth creation, God first created light. God did not create light and the dark. God separated the darkness out. Darkness only happens when something blocks the light. Evil is nothingness, it is absence, in this sense. Heroes reveal to us the "something" after which we strive. Heroes can almost immediately tell the difference between good and evil because they are repelled by evil's nothingness and drawn to the beauty of goodness.

Desmond Tutu saw that beauty. Tutu was a leader in South Africa's anti-apartheid movement and a hero to many. Even in the face of so much evil—discrimination, torture, murder—he still saw in that absence a great potential for good. He wrote, "Each of us has a capacity for great good and that is what makes God say it was well worth the risk to bring us into existence."[3]

Evil is a nothingness that leaves us empty, but out of that emptiness goodness can come. Heroes like Desmond Tutu can see that something *ex nihilo* (out of nothing) reveals the goodness that God begs us to see.

Have you experienced loss? Looking back, have you noticed anything beautiful?

In what ways have you comforted someone who experienced loss?

In your own words, how do you define the difference between good and evil?

SHARING GOODNESS

He has told you, O mortal, what is good;
and what does the LORD require of you
but to do justice, and to love kindness,
and to walk humbly with your God?
Micah 6:8

Heroes are asked to do more than just recognize goodness, and so are we. We are asked to share it. Batman shared goodness by roaming the streets of Gotham City, helping people. For those of us who live outside of comic books, sharing goodness is both simpler and more complicated.

When God looked at creation God saw that it was good. When Jesus talks about goodness, he points us to God. It seems that the direction of goodness flows from creator to creation, and then from creation toward the creator. Goodness is rooted in the relationship between God and creation, and the link is Jesus. In other words, goodness points us to death-defying life—the Resurrection—which is the promise that holds Creator and creation together.

Have you ever asked yourself if you were doing the right thing? Any time I offer my children advice I become curious about whether my "wisdom" will come up in their therapy sessions later! Is what I'm saying good or bad? Thankfully, in the Book of Micah God has already told us what is good: "to do justice, and to love kindness, and to walk humbly with your God" (Micah 6:8).

In that simple phrase, Micah offers us a three-part journey of what it looks like to share goodness. First, we are called to do justice. It means taking a step back, looking at the big picture, and asking difficult questions, such as, "Why are people hungry?" "How can education be more effective?" and "Why does poverty exist?"

Second, we are called to offer works of kindness and mercy, one-on-one acts of kindness like offering a meal, listening to someone who is struggling, or visiting the sick and imprisoned. Mercy and justice go hand in hand. Mercy is feeding someone who is hungry, and justice is asking why he or she is hungry in the first place.

Finally, we must walk humbly with God. On the day of Pentecost, when the people ask Peter what they are supposed to do, he replies, "Repent, and be baptized every one of you in the name of Jesus Christ so that your sins may be forgiven" (Acts 2:38). In other words, humble yourself. Seek forgiveness. Turn toward God. Fall in love with God. Do this and God's promise will be yours.

Jesus teaches this same thing when a lawyer asks, "Who is my neighbor?" Jesus responds with the story of the good Samaritan. Following the parable Jesus asks, "Which of these three, do you think, was a neighbor to the man who fell into the hands of the robbers?" "The one who showed him mercy," the lawyer says. Jesus answers, "Go and do likewise" (Luke 10:36-37).

Do this, and you will live. Lift up those in need. Care for those who have been abused. Bind up the wounded. In other words, love kindness and allow mercy to be the reason your heart beats.

Dorothy Day is a hero for many, and an example of someone who lived out what it means to do justice and love kindness. Day was a key figure in the Catholic Worker Movement, founded in 1933, which fought for those who had little hope during the Great Depression. She is best known for her work on *The Catholic*

Worker, a publication that lifted up stories of those being abused in factories, fought for child labor laws, and maintained pacifism in a time when World War II was just beginning. She was a woman of great faith whose sometimes-jarring opinions cut to the heart of what it means to follow Christ. She often used vilified personalities like Marx and Lenin to discuss loving one's enemies, she spoke out against the church's real estate wealth, and she emphasized the laity's important role in clergy accountability. Justice, kindness, and humility were this hero's superpowers.

What must we do to share goodness? Jesus says to the lawyer that in order for him to recognize eternal life, he must recognize the Samaritan as a brother. He must do justice. Do this and you will live. Jesus says to the rich ruler that in order to understand the gift of eternal life, he must give away the wealth that has captured his heart (Matthew 19:21). He must know generosity. He must love kindness. Do this and you will live. Peter tells the early church that in order to see the gift of eternal life, repent and be baptized. Seek and know forgiveness. Walk humbly with God. Do this, and you will live. What must we do to inherit eternal life? Let us do justice, love kindness, and walk humbly with God so that we may recognize the death-defying life God is offering through Jesus. Do this, and we will live!

What might doing justice look like in your neighborhood?

How can you fall in love with kindness?

What are some of the ways you can walk with God every day?

REAL-LIFE HEROES

Nelson Mandela[4]

Born in South Africa in 1918, Nelson Mandela was the first member of his family to attend school. Since his given name, Rolihlahla, meant "troublemaker," a teacher changed it to Nelson when he was young. Ironically, he became one of the biggest troublemakers in history!

In 1962, during a time when black and white people were segregated in South Africa and black people had very limited rights, Mandela was arrested for traveling without a passport. Because he refused to say that this segregation—known as *apartheid*—was acceptable, he spent twenty-seven years in prison. During that time, he studied nonviolent resistance (Gandhi was a big influence) and became a powerful leader for black South Africans.

After his release in 1990, Mandela advocated for peaceful talks with the president to end apartheid in South Africa, ending many years of subjugation and violence. In 1994, Mandela became the first democratically elected president in the history of South Africa. Affectionately called "Madiba" (the name of his clan), Mandela is considered a hero by most South Africans today. He died in 2013.

No one is born hating another person because of the color of his skin, or his background, or his religion. People must learn to hate, and if they can learn to hate, they can be taught to love, for love comes more naturally to the human heart than its opposite.[5]

The Victory of Good

And remember, I am with you always, to the
end of the age.

Matthew 28:20

Okay, so I will admit that *The Walking Dead* is one of my favorite television series. It's not a family-friendly series, though, so I'm not suggesting you host a church family night viewing party. On the surface, the story follows a group of survivors of a zombie apocalypse who try to cope with the ever-present threat of zombie attacks and the growing danger from other survivors when resources become scarce. One of the most interesting things in the story is its lack of hope. A traditional hero story always has a problem that needs solving. Traditional stories always end happily, but what happens if they don't?

When we hear "they lived happily ever after," we don't seem concerned with what happens next. If the story ends with the bad guys winning, we almost always assume there will be a next chapter. I think the producers of *The Walking Dead* know this. They dangle the possibility of a hopeful ending just enough to keep us watching.

Rick Grimes, the main hero of the series, is in many ways your typical hero. He steps up to be the leader of the group, offers courage in the face of great danger, displays decisive and quick thinking, and protects his people at all costs. With that said, it would be tough to say he is a good guy. Some decisions he makes lead his people into danger, he is slow to offer mercy, and he becomes deaf to people who disagree with him. It is unclear if Rick fights so there will one day be peace or a happy ending. Maybe running from danger is all there is to do, and as a viewer, it's distressing. We always want that happy ending.

Culturally, we are obsessed with the victory of good. When the Empire struck back in the second movie of the original *Star Wars* trilogy, you could assume that there would be a third chapter in the saga. Darth Vader can't win in the end, right? Even the Book of Revelation culminates in a happy ending and a proclamation of Christ's victory. What would we do if the Bible ended with the Crucifixion and we never found out what happened next?

Does good *need* to win in the end? It depends on what it means to win. In the world of heroes, good always triumphs over evil. No matter the odds, heroes are stronger, faster, and wiser than their nemeses. Kryptonite can never keep Superman down for long. Even a bomb couldn't stop Iron Man. And Spider-Man survived a blast of deadly nerve gas to continue fighting crime and saving lives. But this isn't the kind of victory Christ won. Jesus' suffering, death, and resurrection are more than a trilogy with a happy ending. The suffering on the cross was not simply a trial Jesus survived with the help of faith, and neither was the Resurrection a happy ending so we might be satisfied.

Victory over death represents a cosmic shift in God's relationship with creation. No longer does death have the final word in life. But there's a problem. Even if death doesn't have the final answer, it is universal and tragic. God's justifying grace in the person of Jesus Christ was not about God winning. We sing of victory, defeat, and the reign of death ending, but we must not view God's activity on the cross as a mere battle in which God was quick and death was slow.

On the surface, Jesus doesn't seem to be a winner. He led a movement in a small region of the Middle East with twelve devoted followers, and he was put to death at the hands of the government after three years of public ministry. Jesus' victory was not about strength; rather it was born through obedience, humility, trust, and passion. The Gospels announce that Jesus has been raised, meaning that resurrection was not something Jesus did on his own. God, through Christ, in the power of the Holy Spirit, didn't defeat evil; rather, God redeemed and transformed it. Death has been defeated because God revealed the truth that death is empty, and God fulfills the promise to be with us always (Matthew 28:20).

It's not that good wins in the end, the way it happens in traditional hero stories; rather, in the end, there is God. The good news is that God invites us into an eternal relationship through Christ, empowered by the Holy Spirit. It is a self-emptying that offers us a fullness of life.

Deep down we are all repelled by the nothingness of evil. Think of *The Empire Strikes Back*. When Darth Vader had the upper hand at the end of the movie, George Lucas didn't have to tell you that there would be another chapter. We somehow knew the story couldn't end that way. It's not that good wins in the end; rather in the end, there is God. The good news is that God invites us into this eternal relationship through Christ empowered by the Holy Spirit. This is one of the ways in which Jesus redefines what it means to be a hero.

Like other heroes Jesus reveals to us what is good, but the goodness that Jesus reveals is rooted in God. It goes beyond what is pleasing or efficient. Jesus reveals that the goodness in which we are all called to participate is the very presence of God. It is a self-emptying that offers us a fullness of life. There is no struggle between good and evil because the cross reveals that evil is the shadow created when God's light is obscured. Light will always outshine the nothingness with which we too often surround ourselves. Our connection with Christ is the "something" that "nothing" can never take away. There is good, there is evil, and there is God, a God who will stop at nothing (or stops the nothing) to be with us.

If good always wins, how might that change what you have planned for today?

If good always wins, how might that change your perspective when facing adversity?

If good wins in the end, what is there to fear?

Chapter Two

RIGHT, WRONG, AND HOLY

When Peter Parker first took on the superpowers of Spider-Man, he wasn't exactly a proactive superhero. After he was bitten by a radioactive spider, Parker gained super strength and the ability to climb walls and stick to ceilings. After ignoring the opportunity to stop a fleeing thief, Parker discovers that the same thief has returned and killed his uncle. After the murder, these words begin to haunt him: "With great power there must also come—great responsibility."[1] Spider-Man's keen knowledge and firm commitment to right and wrong were born out of this experience and guide everything he does.

Most hero stories present a clear picture of right and wrong in which the heroes have a strict moral code that triumphs over the villain's evil and chaotic worldview. Often Scripture, too, makes a strong distinction between right and wrong, such as in Proverbs 14:14: "The perverse get what their ways deserve, / and the good, what their deeds deserve." This suggests that if you do the right thing, you are rewarded, and if you follow a foolish path, destruction awaits. In Galatians, Paul writes, "Let us not grow weary in doing what is right, for we will reap at harvest time, if we do not give up" (Galatians 6:9).

But Scripture isn't always so clear. During the Sermon on the Mount, Jesus proclaims, "[God] makes his sun rise on the evil and on the good, and sends rain on the righteous and on the unrighteous" (Matthew 5:45). Is doing the right thing always rewarded? Can doing the wrong thing lead to a right outcome? Could doing the right thing actually lead to a wrong ending?

A HERO'S TEMPTATION

*One does not live by bread alone, but by every
word that comes from the mouth of God.*
Matthew 4:3-4

One of the most familiar heroes in the Jewish tradition is Moses. His story follows the path of the traditional hero. It begins with a fantastic origin story. Moses is born to a Hebrew family, is placed in a basket to be rescued from among the reeds, and is taken into the palace as one of Pharaoh's own children. He receives a calling from a voice in a burning bush, goes on a journey to fulfill that calling, fails in that calling nine times, and finally frees the ancient Israelites from slavery so they may begin a covenant with God through the wilderness and into the Promised Land.

This story is so profoundly connected to Jewish identity that Matthew's Gospel goes to great lengths to show that Jesus is like a new Moses. Jesus has a miraculous birth, receives a calling from a voice and the waters of baptism, journeys for forty days in the wilderness, seemingly fails in that calling by being crucified on the cross, only to be raised from the dead to release us from spiritual bondage, offering us God's promise of everlasting life.

Jesus' forty days in the wilderness is a poignant reminder of the ancient Israelites' forty-year wilderness journey. His temptations by the devil offer us vivid examples of right and wrong.

The figure of the devil has its roots in the character named Satan, who is mentioned in the books of Job and Zechariah. The devil is the manifestation of nothingness, which drives him mad because he cannot exist within the grace of God. The devil is a shadow. Shadows are real, but they are only seen when we block the light. So, when we surround ourselves with the light of the Resurrection, in essence, the devil does not exist.

After Jesus fasted for forty days the devil told him, "If you are the Son of God, command these stones to become loaves of bread." Jesus replied, "One does not live by bread alone, but by every word that comes from the mouth of God" (Matthew 4:3-4). In other words, we need bread, and God provides bread, but even bread fails if it is set apart from the eternity that lies in the heart of God.

Then the devil took Jesus to the holy city and set him on the pinnacle of the temple. He said, "If you are the Son of God, throw yourself down; for it is written, 'He will command his angels concerning you.'" Jesus replied, "Again it is written, 'Do not put the Lord your God to the test'" (Matthew 4:6-7).

Running out of options, the devil then took Jesus to a high mountain and promised to give him the kingdoms of the world. Jesus rejected the devil again: "Away with you, Satan! For it is written, 'Worship the Lord your God, and serve only him'" (Matthew 4:10). Jesus didn't talk about kingdoms, but rather the Kingdom, the place where the last shall be first.

Then the light was too bright, and the devil left him.

Like Jesus, even our greatest earthly heroes have foes and circumstances that tempt them away from what they know is right. Our sports heroes are sometimes tempted by performance-enhancing drugs and the idea of being ever bigger and stronger. Iron Man is tempted by alcohol, and he struggles with the help of his friends to overcome that addiction. Odysseus so feared the temptation of the Sirens that he blocked his ears with earplugs and asked his fellow sailors to hold him back should he succumb to their music. And Harry Potter became mesmerized by the vivid image of his dead parents in the mirror of Erised, requiring him to break away and resist the temptation of returning to the mirror and becoming paralyzed by its promises.

Overcoming temptation is one of the passages on a hero's journey. Jesus takes this idea to new heights when he refuses all temptation, chooses right over wrong, and stays focused on his own journey to conquer death and save humanity.

In what ways do you think Moses and Jesus were similar? In what ways were they different?

Which temptation of Jesus in the wilderness do you think may have been the most difficult for Jesus to resist? Why?

What temptations do you struggle with? How do you cope with those temptations?

SUPERHEROES

Spider-Man[2]

Comic

Publisher: Marvel Comics
Created by: Stan Lee and Steve Ditko
First appeared: *Amazing Fantasy* #15, August 1962

Character

Alter ego: Peter Parker
Species: Human
Hometown: Queens, New York
Team: The Avengers
Powers:
Genius-level intellect
Super strength, speed, and agility
Ability to cling to most surfaces
Spider sense, which warns of incoming danger
Equipment: Web-shooters
Enemies:
The Green Goblin
Doctor Octopus
Sandman

Interesting fact

Martin Goodman, the head of Marvel during Spider-Man's initial development, strongly discouraged the idea of Spider-Man because people hate spiders.

SUPERHEROES

Origin

After he was bitten by a radioactive spider, high school student Peter Parker gained the abilities of a spider. Rather than use his new powers responsibly, he instead decides to become a wrestler and earn money for himself. When a robber shoots his Uncle Ben, Peter tracks down the criminal to bring him to justice, only to learn that the shooter was in fact the same man Peter had encountered committing another crime, but Peter chose not to act. From that day forward, Peter chose to use his abilities responsibly as Spider-Man.

Heroic moment

Peter Parker, the alter ego of Spider-Man, comes face to face with Sandman, the man who actually killed Peter's Uncle Ben. Setting aside his anger and vengeful rage, Peter listens to Sandman's story and chooses to forgive him. Sandman is sorrowful and apologetic as he turns to dust and flies away.[3]

SATAN AS VILLAIN

The LORD said to Satan, "The LORD rebuke
you, O Satan! The LORD who has chosen Jerusalem
rebuke you! Is not this man a brand plucked from
the fire?"

Zechariah 3:2

Satan is an intriguing character throughout the Christian tradition. Some consider Satan to be an angel gone rogue. Others see him as the chief of demons or a spiritual force of wickedness. Still others see Satan as a mythological creature, absence made manifest, a representation of the dark side of human free will, or simply a scapegoat. In order to better understand this villain of all villains, let's turn to Scripture.

In the Bible, Satan evolves from God's accuser, to oppositional spiritual force on earth, to leader of demons with almost unmatched evil power. As persecution of the church begins to grow, there emerges an increasing need to explain evil within the world. As a result, the character of the devil gains more and more power in theological writings.

Satan first appears in the Old Testament when "Satan stood up against Israel, and incited David to count the people of Israel" (1 Chronicles 21:1). Curiously, there is no backstory or footnote or flashback to explain who this Satan character is; therefore, we can probably assume that the audience knew of the character.

The Old Testament books of Job and Zechariah include stories that use the Hebrew word *ha-satan*. This word can be translated as "the accuser" or "the adversary," but usually it just appears as Satan. Sometimes this adversary is human, someone who stands against another individual or group; other times, God sends a heavenly adversary to oppose someone working against God's will. The character of the devil found in the New Testament, as in Jesus' temptation, is not necessarily the same character as *ha-satan* found in the Old Testament.

At places in the Old Testament, Satan is given the limited ability to influence humanity. For example, Satan influences David and is an accuser in Psalm 109:6 and Zechariah 3:1. However, the idea of Satan, accuser or otherwise, is not a prominent theme within Old Testament literature. Evil is not usually attributed to a separate spiritual being.

In the New Testament, Satan performs a different role in each kind of literature: gospel, epistle, and apocalyptic. In the Gospels, Satan—now called the devil—is a human-like spiritual force outside the presence of God, having power and influence in the world in opposition to the work of God. In the Epistles, Satan is a spiritual force that Christians are called to resist, and they have some success at it. The character of the devil continues to grow in strength over time, until in the apocalyptic Book of Revelation, his power is nearly equivalent to God's. Revelation suggests that the devil brings wrath upon the earth, devouring and conquering humanity to the point at which God must finally intervene. A great battle ensues, and the devil is eventually bound and thrown into eternal damnation.

In our superhero stories, we look to villains to symbolize what we loathe and fear. In comic books and movies, Spider-Man represents things we value: justice, order, law, and getting a date for the prom. In his teenage way, he fights criminals and restores order and peace. The Green Goblin is Spider-Man's archenemy and greatest villain. He represents the opposite of Spider-Man's virtues. Using Halloween props and themes, the Green Goblin promotes chaos, disorder, and anarchy. He is the ultimate wrong to Spider-Man's right.

When Jesus finds himself tempted by the devil, he is faced with a nemesis who embodies everything he is not, that is, the total absence of light, goodness, and love. While superheroes must use their super powers to defeat their enemies, Jesus' victory over Satan comes from his very being. The light of Christ cancels out the empty shadow that the devil represents.

The Bible describes differing versions of Satan. How do you account for those differences?

Which version of Satan rings the truest to you? Why?

Do you personally believe in Satan? If you do, describe your version of Satan.

BREAKING THE RULES

*The sabbath was made for humankind, and
not humankind for the sabbath.*

Mark 2:27

We think of our heroes as fighting for what is right, but sometimes that means breaking the rules. On December 1, 1955,

47

in Montgomery, Alabama, Rosa Parks refused to give up her seat on the bus to a white passenger, defying the law at that time. Parks was arrested. Later, she reported:

> People always say that I didn't give up my seat because I was tired, but that isn't true. I was not tired physically, or no more tired than I usually was at the end of a working day. I was not old, although some people have an image of me as being old then. I was forty-two. No, the only tired I was, was tired of giving in.[4]

Rosa Parks's refusal to give in was a powerful example of what the gospel looks like in action. Jesus said to the crowd, "You have heard that it was said, 'An eye for an eye and a tooth for a tooth.' But I say to you, Do not resist an evildoer. But if anyone strikes you on the right cheek, turn the other also" (Matthew 5:38-39). Parks refused to react with violence, and she refused to be moved. In the process she was obstructing the authority granted to the bus driver, as well as the laws of segregation and discrimination. She was breaking the rules for all the right reasons.

Of course, rules are important in society. They keep us safe, help ensure equality, promote fairness in the marketplace, and bring clarity to our shared lives together. Without rules, it would be easy to become lost, exhausted, and reactive.

When I was growing up, my friends and I would play football in the street between our houses. We would always spend the first fifteen minutes deciding on the rules. You might think that sounds excessive, but we knew from experience that it was necessary. Without a clear agreement that the mailboxes were out-of-bounds and that you were down after two hands touched you, the afternoon usually would end badly, with words we hoped our mothers didn't hear and punches we hoped our fathers wouldn't see.

As important as rules are, they aren't perfect and never will be. When the rules breed injustice, abuse, and discrimination, we have to ask who is making the rules, why they are making them, and for what purpose.

Jesus gained a reputation as a rebel against the religious and governing authorities, but to say he broke the rules isn't precisely correct. Early in Mark's Gospel, Jesus and the disciples were going through the fields and picking grain on the Sabbath. The Pharisees questioned why Jesus was permitting such an unlawful act. Jesus replied, "Have you never read what David did when he and his companions were hungry and in need of food? . . . The sabbath was made for humankind, and not humankind for the sabbath" (Mark 2:25, 27). Here, Jesus grounded his position in Scripture and questioned the humanity of the rule in question. Like Rosa Parks, Jesus knew what the Law instructed, but he allowed the genuine human need in question—the disciples' hunger—to supersede the letter of the Law.

Jesus didn't simply distinguish between right and wrong. His ministry was not just about upholding what was right and condemning what was wrong. He sought to understand and amplify the Law, bringing to mind what motivates us to do wrong rather than focusing only on the wrongdoing itself. In Jesus, the words of Jeremiah came to life. Our law was written on our hearts, not just on a piece of stone. Jesus found good where the Law found fault, as in the field where hungry disciples plucked grain on the sabbath and law-minded observers called foul.

Julio Diaz, a social worker in the Bronx, would commute daily in and out of town. One night, as he got off of the subway, a teenager approached him brandishing a knife asking for his wallet. He quickly surrendered his wallet, but as the young man was walking away, Julio called out to him, "If you're going to be out here all night robbing folks, here, take my coat." Surprised, the young man asked why he was doing this. Julio replied, "If you're willing to risk your freedom for a few dollars, you must really need it. All I was going to do was grab a bite to eat. Want to join me?" And he did.[5] This is what the gospel looks like in action. He refused to react with violence, and he just might have changed someone's life. Julio had every right to call the police and resist having his wallet stolen. Instead he chose to give and to feed.

Superheroes such as Spider-Man seek to maintain law and order, but the work of Jesus was deeper than that. Law and order serves one purpose, but there may be other paths to goodness, as with Julio Diaz. Jesus' work was about understanding what the Law really means, opening it up to wider interpretations, and bringing it to its fulfillment on the cross.

Do you think we're ever justified in breaking the law? Under what circumstances do you feel it's justified? Under what circumstances do you think it may not be justified?

The text names Rosa Parks and people who disregarded the law on principle. What other people can you think of, and what did they do?

What laws, if any, do you feel supersede the laws of our government? Are we ever justified in breaking these?

REAL-LIFE HEROES

Harriet Tubman[6]

Harriet Tubman (c.1820–1913) was born a slave in Maryland in 1820. She left her family behind and escaped to the north in 1849. She became famously known as a "conductor" on the Underground Railroad, a network of anti-slavery activists and safe houses that helped individuals and families escape to freedom. Tubman was an abolitionist, a humanitarian, and also a spy for the Union army during the Civil War. Even though there was a bounty on her head, Tubman made multiple missions into the South to escort her family and more than seventy other slaves to freedom in the North. At great personal expense and sacrifice, Tubman devoted her life to helping slaves escape the evils of slavery and working for a better life for all.

I said to the Lord, I'm going to hold steady on to you, and I know you will see me through.[7]

THE TRIUMPH OF STORY

Go and do likewise.
Luke 10:37

The battle between right and wrong is an important part of superhero comics and movies, but something else is more important: the story. In the story of Spider-Man, we follow the adventures and misadventures of Peter Parker as he fights the forces of evil while at the same time waging the battles of a typical teenager.

The Christian calling is not about being right, and it certainly isn't about constantly being wrong. Our role is to continue God's story, and continuing that story means doing what is holy.

You see, the Bible is more than a rule book. It's a script that leaves room for improvisation. The Bible doesn't tell us everything we want to know; we have to figure it out according to how we have been shaped and formed in our faith journey.

Once there was a concert pianist who was performing Chopin to an exclusive audience. During the concert, a small child in the first few rows began making a scene. "Shhh!" whispered the parents. "Sit down!" The child leaped out of her seat and headed for the stage. The pianist had a choice to make. He could stop playing and send the child back to her parents. He could relinquish the piano to her and leave. Or he could get up from his seat and give the child permission to play, which is what he finally decided to do. While she played, he stood behind her, placed his hands on either side of hers, and improvised a melody to fit what her small hands were banging out. As Christians, we are called to respond creatively so the story of God continues. It may not be right or wrong, but it may be holy.

Sometimes the difference between right and wrong isn't clear at all. In some cases, the choice is made by a hero whose quick thinking and improvisation save the day and save lives. After their car skidded off the road and landed upside down in a snowy ravine, a couple and their four children found themselves stranded. Night was approaching, and along with it subzero temperatures. Armed only with the winter coats they would wear on their day trip, they faced a very dangerous situation. Together, the couple came up with an idea. They built a bonfire and heated some rocks. Then they placed those rocks inside their car's spare tire. This created a heater they could place inside to warm the car, keeping all six of them safe all night until help could arrive. On that frigid evening, there could have been no more holy warmth.

Christians are called to do more than follow the rules. If this is not our calling, then we could live perfectly happy inside the four walls of our churches being careful never to break any laws. Jesus taught that the gospel is more than right versus wrong. When a lawyer quizzed him and then offered a response, Jesus first said, "You have given the right answer; do this, and you will live" (Luke 10:28). When the lawyer pressed him, Jesus told a story:

> "A man was going down from Jerusalem to
> Jericho, and fell into the hands of robbers, who
> stripped him, beat him, and went away, leaving
> him half dead. Now by chance a priest was going
> down that road; and when he saw him, he passed
> by on the other side. So likewise a Levite, when

*he came to the place and saw him, passed by on
the other side. But a Samaritan while traveling
came near him; and when he saw him, he was
moved with pity. He went to him and bandaged
his wounds, having poured oil and wine on them.
Then he put him on his own animal, brought him
to an inn, and took care of him. The next day he
took out two denarii, gave them to the innkeeper,
and said, 'Take care of him; and when I come
back, I will repay you whatever more you spend.'
Which of these three, do you think, was a neighbor
to the man who fell into the hands of the robbers?"
He said, "The one who showed him mercy." Jesus
said to him, "Go and do likewise."*

Luke 10:30-37

Following Christ is not about being right or wrong; it's about continuing God's story through holiness of living. Holiness is our calling as Christians. Yes, there is right. Rules help us understand the boundaries and offer order to our daily life. Yes, there is wrong, sin that leads to oppression, damaging one's own soul, the breaking of relationships, and profit over people. The gospel calls us to an even higher calling than discerning right from wrong. We are called to do that which is holy, so that the eternal life of Christ might be shared here, now, and forever. Jesus is a hero not because he fights for what is right and resists what is wrong. Life is not a series of choices between right and wrong; rather life is about our relationship with God and with one another. Jesus redefined the rules and brought them to completion so that we might be a holy people. There is right, there is wrong, and the Resurrection reveals that there is holy.

Do you agree that the Bible is a script leaving room for improvisation? In what ways is this description accurate? In what ways might it be inaccurate?

Are there times when the Bible is more a rule book than a script? Explain.

How would you define holiness? How do you see it applying to your own life?

Chapter Three

US, THEM, AND THE BODY OF CHRIST

On October 21, 2016, the United Nations announced that it would make Wonder Woman an honorary ambassador in support of their goal to achieve gender equality and empower all women and girls. The announcement was met with great fanfare, and October 21 was declared to be "Wonder Woman Day."

Not long after, a concerned group of United Nations staffers circulated a petition in protest of the superhero's honorary title. The petition claimed that the Wonder Woman character was "not culturally encompassing or sensitive" and that she was "an inappropriate choice at a time 'when the headline news in United States and the world is the objectification of women and girls.'"[1] By December 13, 2016, Wonder Woman had lost her honorary title and no longer served as a symbolic figure for the United Nations' mission for women.

Though she turned out to be divisive in her United Nations role—and became a kind of fallen hero in the process—Wonder Woman's goal in her comic-book realm is to unite rather than divide. When conflicts arise that pit "us" versus "them," she seeks ways to bring the two sides together into a common "we." Some of our real-life heroes do the same thing. And in our churches we find that sharing the body of Christ is one way we celebrate the heroic and uniting presence of Jesus in our communities, both large and small.

WHO ARE "WE"?

God has so arranged the body, giving the
greater honor to the inferior member, that there
may be no dissension within the body, but the
members may have the same care for one another.
1 Corinthians 12:24-25

When we lift up our cultural heroes and assume they represent everyone and everything, we can make a grave error. Certainly there are some common goals and interests we share across cultures, but who gets to decide what it means, for example, to be American? Does being an American have something to do with the food we eat, the music we enjoy, or the way we interact? In other words, Superman fights for "Truth, justice, and the American

Way," but this doesn't play well in Russia. Let's shrink the sphere down a bit. What does it mean to be a part of your community?

Heroes help us define our culture and celebrate who we are. When I was growing up in south Louisiana, examples of vibrant and unique culture were everywhere. Jazz music poured out onto the streets, crawfish boils were a common weekend neighborhood gathering, and home football games ruled the day. In those days, just as now, heroes help us define and appreciate what it means to be a people. Louis Armstrong was a gifted and charismatic musician who embodied much of what New Orleans is all about. Even the airport is named for him. His music is part of what it means to be from New Orleans. Who are the regional heroes in your city? Whose personality sets the standard for what it means to be a part of your community?

Even though we all have characters and events and symbols that unite us, we must be careful how we use the word *we*. One of my pet peeves is when preachers use the word *we* in sermons: "When we read this Scripture . . ." or "When we look at the world . . ." What if I'm not thinking what you're thinking? It's hard to keep an audience attentive if you're assuming what's going on in their heads. Not everyone who has gathered for worship is looking at the world through the same lens.

Even our heroes don't see eye to eye all the time. Marvel's *Captain America: Civil War* was the highest grossing film in 2016, raking in $1.153 billion. One of the reasons for its popularity is how the different heroes of the Marvel Universe (Iron Man, Captain America, Spider-Man, and others) responded differently to a common crisis. At stake was how superheroes should be held accountable. One side wanted to unite under a common banner for accountability. The other side felt that a common banner with that much power would ultimately lead to corruption.

What's a fan to do? Do I choose Iron Man and accountability, or do I side with Captain America against possible corruption? Is one clearly right and the other clearly wrong? Do I claim that one side is "us," and the other side "them," and if so, what is my responsibility to "them"?

What they're really discussing is trust. Iron Man doesn't trust the other heroes, and Captain America doesn't trust the hierarchy. I wonder how different the movie would have been if they recognized the root of their disagreement, but who wants superheroes to shake hands and agree? I'd rather see them fight, and apparently so would millions of others. I wonder how our disagreements might end up if we could recognize the illness rather than acting out the symptoms. The way we frame an argument is just as important, and maybe more important, than the argument itself.

How can we make a frame that's sturdy and clearly defined, but flexible enough for the Holy Spirit to move? It begins with how we define *we*. When we come to the table, are we broken? When we gather together, are we speaking the same language? When we meet with our brothers and sisters, what lens are we using to interpret the world? If Jesus, when he broke the bread and poured the wine, could gather at the same table both Simon the Zealot (who wanted to overthrow the government) and Matthew the tax collector (who worked for the government) then maybe there's hope for "us" and "them" to become "we."

Who are some heroes in your city, state, or region? What does their fame in your area tell us about the place where you live?

It seems that each superhero has a slightly different "right" they are fighting for. Based on what you've learned in this book and elsewhere, which superhero's "right" do you most agree with?

From what we read in the Bible, how would you describe Jesus' community? What did his community tell us about Jesus?

SUPERHEROES

Wonder Woman[2]

Comic

Publisher: DC Comics
Created By: William Moulton Marston and Harry G. Peter
First Appeared: *All Star Comics* #8, October 1941

Character

Alter Ego: Princess Diana of Themyscira; Diana Prince
Species: Amazonian
Homeland: Themyscira
Team: Justice League
Powers:
Super Strength, speed, and durability
Flight
Master Combatant
Equipment:
The Lasso of Truth (which prevents those in its grasp from
    telling a lie)
Indestructible bracelets
Enemies:
Circe
Ares
Cheetah
Doctor Poison

SUPERHEROES

Interesting fact

William Marston, the creator of Wonder Woman, also invented the lie detector test.

Origin

Diana was born on Themyscira, the island of the Amazons. Her mother, the leader of the Amazons, had told Diana that she was molded from clay and brought to life, but in reality, she is the daughter of Zeus and was hidden on Themyscira for her protection. When outside threats intrude on the peace of her home, she journeys into the world of man, bringing with her the ideals of justice, equality, peace, and love to guide her.

Heroic moment

Wonder Woman made history in 2017 as the very first female character to headline a solo live-action movie. She appears as a powerful woman in defiance of evil, despotic men as she moves through the trenches of World War I and deflects the bullets of German soldiers. In her efforts to stop the war, Wonder Woman works to create communion where there is division.

TAKE ME TO YOUR LEADER

I have called you friends, because I have made
known to you everything that I have heard from
my Father. You did not choose me but I chose you.
John 15:15-16

"Take me to your leader" is a phrase sometimes used in science fiction cartoons when two different groups meet, such as a cadre of aliens landing on earth and encountering humans for the first time. The line is often intended humorously, but it has serious meaning.

We look to leaders to understand people because leaders often represent what it means to be a member of a community. In doing so, they demonstrate an important part of being a hero.

Susan B. Anthony is seen as a hero of the women's suffrage movement because she represented the tenacity, dedication, and spirit of the movement itself. And although there were other heroes who dedicated their lives to the civil rights movement, Dr. Martin Luther King Jr.'s commitment to nonviolence and the tragedy of his martyrdom elevated King to become a symbol of the movement as a whole. Heroes seem to have an ordained ability to lead and an anointed sense that they are set apart to *be* the movement they carry.

As charismatic and assertive as heroes can be, they accomplish little without followers. Although heroes never fear to step out in front and lead the charge, heroic leaders know they can't go alone. The secret weapon for any hero is the first and second follower.

Picture a typical 1980s teen movie. When the shy boy finally realizes that he loves the girl, he hurries to meet her at the pep rally before the quarterback can invite her to prom. He runs up in front of the entire school and professes his love for her. There is a silence that seems to last for an eternity, and then, from the corner of the gym, someone begins a slow clap. Then another joins in, and another, until the entire student body is cheering the newfound lovers (to the quarterback's chagrin). The shy boy has become a hero, but without the first follower who showed his affirmation with the slow clap, and the second follower who joined in, the scene would have been painfully awkward, and the boy might have left defeated and ostracized from the community.

And so we can see that the hero isn't much without the first and second follower. I think this is why Jesus chose the disciples so early in his ministry. Jesus was walking along the Sea of Galilee when he called out to Simon, Andrew, James, and John. They stopped what they were doing and decided to follow Jesus.

I've always been fascinated by the kind of charisma Jesus must have had to be able to recruit followers by simply saying, "Follow me." (I've tried saying, "Clean up your room" to my children, and it quickly becomes obvious that I lack the same charismatic appeal.) After he called this handful of disciples, it took only three verses for Jesus' mission to spread around Galilee, the Decapolis, Jerusalem, Judea, and beyond the Jordan (Matthew 4:23-25). The movement spread quickly, but what if Peter, Andrew, James, and John had said no?

Heroes need followers, and followers have a wide variety of gifts. Paul is right in saying that there are many gifts through the one Holy Spirit (1 Corinthians 12:4). Often when I talk to people about discovering their calling in serving Christ, they get stuck in thinking that the only way to serve is to preach, teach an evening class, or spend a week serving on a global mission team. When thinking about calling, I invite people to think about three things: passion, joy, and fulfillment.

Having a passion for something doesn't necessarily mean that it's fun. Passion is a suffering love. It is something that you would gladly suffer for. I would consider many parents to be passionate about their children, meaning that in the midst of tragedy, parents wouldn't hesitate to put themselves in harm's way to protect their children. Firefighters, police officers, and members of the military are passionate about serving, in that they run toward danger so the rest of us don't have to. I've met musicians practicing and playing for hours at a time for pennies because they believe in the importance of music. What are you passionate about?

Joy is closely related to passion, or suffering love. Joy isn't always a happy feeling. It certainly wasn't when Jesus said, "Blessed are you when people hate you, and when they exclude you, revile you, and defame you on account of the Son of Man. Rejoice in that day and *leap for joy*, for surely your reward is great in heaven" (Luke 6:22-23a, emphasis mine). Joy is the steadfast assurance that God is with you. It is the knowledge that whatever happens, God is there.

Finally, answering your calling gives a sense of fulfillment. It's almost as if the air around you is lighter than before. In ministry, there are certainly difficult days when everything feels heavier than it ought to be. Counseling a couple going through divorce, offering words of hope when a loved one is dying, and facilitating a discussion in the midst of division isn't easy, but there are days when I've experienced a fulfillment beyond words. I can't explain the fullness of baptizing a baby who finally was released from the NICU, saying a prayer at a long-awaited wedding, or seeing someone graduate from the homeless shelter knowing that his future is brighter than his past.

Calling allows us to share our passion, discover our joy, and experience all the fullness that abundant life has to offer. Heroes cultivate this calling in the people around them. Heroes help us see calling in action, and they know the vision they see is nothing without disciples who know they have a place.

Jesus spent his life teaching, healing, and revealing the miraculous; but he also empowered those around him to do the same and even greater works. It's amazing and humbling to hear Jesus say his followers will do even greater things than he accomplished, but Jesus is a hero and that's what heroes do. Yes, they step out and move toward the vision God has offered; but as they walk, they make sure their followers grow stronger, so that those who were once following begin to outstep the hero himself. On Jesus' last night with his disciples he offered them the beauty of calling:

> *I do not call you servants any longer, because the servant does not know what the master is doing; but I have called you friends, because I have made known to you everything that I have heard from my Father. You did not choose me but I chose you. And I appointed you to go and bear fruit, fruit that will last, so that the Father will give you whatever you ask him in my name. I am giving you these commands so that you may love one another.*
>
> *John 15:15-17*

Christ led the way, and he encourages us to do the same. Not only that, he says that we are servants no longer, but are friends! Finally, he commands us to go out and bear fruit that will last—fruit that will last longer than Jesus' earthly ministry, fruit that will outlive you and me, fruit that will remain until heaven and earth are one.

If someone wants to know who the heroes of the church are, point them to the people who are the hands and feet of Christ.

Who are some leaders in your community? Is there a difference between a leader and a hero? If so, what is it?

What's the importance of followers? Are there times when it's better to be a follower than a leader?

Have there been times when you were the first or second follower? If there have been, describe them.

THE FALLEN HERO

When they saw him, they worshiped him; but some doubted.

Matthew 28:17

For many years, home run hitter and first baseman Mark McGwire was my hero. As a child I loved the St. Louis Cardinals, and I idolized Mark McGwire because I spent my summers playing first base in youth baseball. In 1998, McGwire shattered one of baseball's most famous records by hitting 70 home runs in a season.

Three years later, in the final year of his career, I was thrilled to see McGwire hit career home runs 565 and 566 in person in Houston, Texas. I am not too proud to tell you that I wept. I couldn't believe that I got to see my hero in action.

I was so moved that my mother bought me an oil painting of Big Mac hitting his famous record-breaking home run against the Cubs in 1998. I even made the mistake of placing the painting above the mantle after my wife and I got married. Needless to say, the painting was moved. It's now behind a bookshelf in the study. For me, Mark McGwire could do no wrong.

And then there was the scandal. McGwire was caught using performance-enhancing drugs. My idol and hero had fallen.

It is so very interesting what happens to us when our heroes fall. For me, it was as if I was going through the stages of grief. At first I denied that it happened. Obviously something went wrong, and the tests must be false positives. Then I slipped into anger. I would think to myself, "How could they say that about the person whose rookie card I keep in a protective glass case?" Sometimes I would be angry at McGwire himself, thinking, "How could you do this?" Next I began to bargain. I mean, even if he had used drugs, he still had to hit a fastball, right? It's not like the drugs helped his hand-eye coordination. Then there was a great sadness that I had devoted so much time and energy watching his swing and collecting his baseball cards. In a way, his failure felt like my failure. Finally, I came to a point of accepting the whole thing. I still have his rookie card and the oil painting, and I realize that baseball is just a game. It is a beautiful game, but a game nonetheless.

We identify so closely with our heroes' accomplishments that their failures and shortcomings feel like ours as well. It is no surprise that the Bible says nothing about the disciples the day after Jesus was crucified. I picture them running away and hiding behind closed doors. I imagine their thoughts. *If Jesus is dead, then how can we trust what he taught? If he isn't what he said he was, then am I who he said I am?*

We fall when our heroes fall, because we are reminded of the unresolved mistakes in our own story. The good news is that Scripture isn't silent for long.

Have you ever had a hero who disappointed you? What did the person do, and why were you disappointed?

When a hero falls, what do you think is a positive and constructive response?

What do you think the disciples may have done the day Jesus was crucified? What did it show about them?

STILL HAVEN'T FOUND WHAT I'M LOOKING FOR

"This is the one about whom it is written,
'See, I am sending my messenger ahead of you,
who will prepare your way before you.'"
Luke 7:27

When our heroes fall, we might think we've made a mistake in following them at all, but in doing so we ignore what Jesus came to show us.

When John the Baptist was in prison, he sent a message asking if Jesus was the one to come. Instead of offering a simple yes, Jesus said, "Go and tell John what you have seen and heard: the blind receive their sight, the lame walk, the lepers are cleansed, the deaf hear, the dead are raised, the poor have good news brought to them" (Luke 7:22).

Scripture doesn't say why John asked the question, or whether Jesus' answer was what John wanted to hear; but the exchange does reveal the power of misguided expectations. In spite of what John may have expected, Jesus did not come to establish a new nation, politic, or school of thought. Jesus' answer to John offers a clue to what we should look to in a hero. He simply said, in effect, "What do you see?"

When you look at your church, what do you see? I'm not talking about the way the people dress, what cars they drive, or where they live, though these are all excellent questions to consider. More to the point, how does your church fulfill the vision that God has offered? Put another way, if your church disappeared overnight, who in the community would know that it was gone?

A few years ago, several churches came together to offer a "U2charist"—a communion service using only music by the band U2—in the middle of downtown Shreveport, Louisiana. We hoped the event would attract folks who were unfamiliar with the church, young adults looking for a new worship experience, and others drawn to the live music and willing to hang out with us for a free concert around Jesus' table. We spent months planning the event, getting the media just right, and rehearsing the musicians.

On the one hand, the event was a smashing success. The music was spot-on, hundreds of people came, and our guest speaker offered a convicting word. On the other hand, I remember looking at the crowd and seeing mostly people from area churches. Our goal hadn't been for the church to celebrate itself. The droves of outsiders we had hoped for never arrived. The bars were filled just as they would be if we hadn't been there.

Yet, something powerful happened at the event that I had not expected. During the gathering, several homeless people wandered in. At first they hung out by the entrance, unsure if they were welcome. Then, at the end of the concert, as we packed up the leftover Communion elements, one of the homeless men had the courage to approach the table and ask, "Can I have that?" There was a brief silence after the question. Running through my mind was the shame of not having offered the bread and juice to them before packing it away. Thankfully, someone else jumped in. "Of course," she said, and we handed over everything we had left.

As the man walked away, the lesson continued. He shared what we had given to him with the rest of the people hanging out by the entrance.

Who was the hero at the U2charist event? Maybe the clergy felt heroic, in that they were doing something new and different and were creating an opportunity for new people to encounter the church. But in the end the hero wasn't a pastor. It was the homeless man who dared to ask for the leftover Communion bread and juice, then shared it with his hungry and thirsty friends. He united two communities the way a hero is uniquely equipped to do.

That hero, like Jesus, taught us the power of misguided expectations. Many expected Jesus to be an earthly king who would chase the Roman oppressors away. When he was crucified, even the disciples became silent as they wrestled with what it all meant.

If they had been paying attention, they would have realized that it wasn't just Jesus who was nailed to the cross that day. It was our expectations rooted in the hope for power, influence, violence, and selfishness. It was the desire to have a strong "us" at the expense of a weak "them."

Jesus came so we might realize that there is no "us" and "them." Sometimes it takes a broken body to find our wholeness.

If your church disappeared overnight, what do you think would result?

Can you think of an example from your own life when you were expecting one outcome, got a different outcome instead, and the result was positive? Describe it.

Do you feel there is no "us" and "them"? Can you imagine a situation in which this would actually be helpful?

REAL-LIFE HEROES

Anne Frank[3]

During the German occupation of the Netherlands in World War II, thirteen-year old Anne Frank went into hiding in a secret annex above an office where she and her family stayed from 1942 to 1944. Fearing capture, the Jewish family hid in careful silence in the small space with the help of several friends working in the offices below. During that time, the young Anne documented their lives in her diary. Nazis discovered and arrested the family in 1944. After the house was raided, one of the helpers, Miep Gies, discovered Anne's diary and hid it in her desk until the end of the war, when she returned it to Otto Frank, Anne's father. Since then, the diary has been translated into sixty-seven languages and has served as a window into history and source of inspiration for millions of readers.

> It's a wonder I haven't abandoned all my ideals, they seem so absurd and impractical. Yet I cling to them because I still believe, in spite of everything, that people are truly good at heart.
> It's utterly impossible for me to build my life on a foundation of chaos, suffering and death. I see the world being slowly transformed into a wilderness, I hear the approaching thunder that, one day, will destroy us too, I feel the suffering of millions. And yet, when I look up at the sky, I somehow feel that everything will change for the better, that this cruelty too shall end, that peace and tranquility will return once more.[4]

GOD IN ME, GOD IN US

Surely the LORD is in this place—and I did not know it!

Genesis 28:16

Heroes reveal to us what it means to be part of a community. They show us what it means to be "us."

Wonder Woman grew up in a community of Amazon warriors, isolated on an island. She experienced strong but limited community at the beginning of her life, and then later, when she discovered the wider world, her concept of community expanded to include all of it.

In the Bible, the idea of community is related to the concept of God in us. The author of 1 John makes a bold claim: "No one has ever seen God; if we love one another, God lives in us, and his love is perfected in us" (1 John 4:12). Scripture contains a long history of people experiencing God's presence.

In the garden, Adam and Eve experienced God's presence as someone who walked with them. When they hid after eating the forbidden fruit, Scripture says, "They heard the sound of the LORD God walking in the garden at the time of the evening breeze, and the man and his wife hid themselves from the presence of the LORD God among the trees of the garden" (Genesis 3:8). Adam and Eve had an intimate relationship with God. The presence of the Lord walked with them and talked with them.

As we continue through Scripture, each character in God's story seems to have a different experience of God's presence.

For Abraham, God's presence is mysterious, not because God's presence is hard to define, but because Abraham is rarely offered any answers as to why God was asking him to do things. And yet Abraham followed where God was calling him, and through him two great nations were born. I get the sense that Abraham's experience of God was something like a gut feeling. Sometimes I don't know why God is calling me to a place, but I get the feeling that it is a good thing. Has this been your experience?

Jacob, Abraham's grandson, had quite a different experience with God. In fact, Jacob didn't really have a relationship with God. When he talked about God, he would say, "Your God." This would be as though you were praying the Lord's Prayer, and instead of saying, "Our Father," you can only mutter, "Your Father." Jacob's first experience of God was when he was on the run from his brother. He was alone in the wilderness using a rock as a pillow. In other words, he literally had hit rock bottom, and that was the place where he had a vision of God. Jacob said, "Surely the LORD is in this place—and I did not know it!" (Genesis 28:16).

Then we get to Moses, and again, his experience of God was different. Moses knew that he was one of God's people, but we don't know what kind of relationship he had with God until he ran away from Egypt. Can you relate to this? Maybe your family went to church, but you never felt a deep connection with God until you were out on your own. Moses' experience was not a passive one. He saw a burning bush in the distance, and he sought it out.

I don't offer these stories to say that you have to hit rock bottom or climb a mountain or follow your instincts in order to experience God, but these stories reveal that God shows himself in the way we need to see him. God uses a language we can understand so that we might respond. To prove this, God assumed our humanity in the person of Jesus and walked with us.

Jesus, the Word of God, used our words. He ate our food and gave it a new and holy meaning. He suffered our sin so that we might be redeemed. He loved the outcast, got angry with the religious, lived among the poor, and healed the sick. Because of Jesus, being connected with God is no longer about seeing God up there and out there, but seeing God in the face of one another. Through love, God's presence dwells within us.

What did Christ reveal about who we are together, as a community? When you join the church I serve, we ask that you support the church with your presence—showing up. It's like the song many of us learned in vacation Bible school: "I am the church! You are the church! We are the church together!" Being part of a church is about showing up, but not so that the pews are filled for the pastor's report, or that the offering plate meets the needs of the finance committee. It's about two things.

First, we carry around with us a picture of who God is, and as we have seen in the stories of Moses and Jacob and Gideon that presence is particular and peculiar. In other words, if we only knew Moses, we would think that we have to climb the mountain to see God. If only Gideon showed up, we might think we have to hide in order to find God. In the same way, when we aren't with others in a faith community, our picture of God is diminished and not as full as it needs to be. The more people who gather together in worship to pray and sing and give and hear the proclamation, the more detailed our picture of God will be.

Second, it's about learning how to love. If you get two people in a room, each one of them is going to disagree with the other about something: sports, politics, favorite color, you name it. God dwells in the person with whom you disagree. What picture of God do you reveal? How does your presence reveal God's presence? In a real sense, no one has seen God apart from seeing God in one another.

Christ is our true hero because he revealed what it means to be connected to one another. As Paul puts it, "There is no longer Jew or Greek, there is no longer slave or free, there is no longer male and female; for all of you are one in Christ Jesus" (Galatians 3:28).

Heroes reveal what it means to be part of a community. They embody how the community sees itself. Sometimes our heroes are tragic because they have fallen away from who the community aspires to be, or they no longer meet the expectations we place upon them. Christ did fall, carrying the weight of our misguided expectations of the salvation we think we needed, but he rose again to reveal that our unity in the body of Christ is stronger than disagreement, prejudice, division, and even death itself. God created us all to be together. There is us, there is them, and there is the body of Christ in which we are all invited.

Adam and Eve, Abraham, Jacob, and Moses all had different experiences of God. What is your experience of God? What experience of God do you aspire to?

"God uses a language we can understand." Do you think this is true? Why or why not?

In your opinion, why is Christ our true hero? What does that mean?

Chapter Four

Have, Have-Not, and the Kingdom of God

Our heroes most often give us clear examples of what is good, what is right, and what it means to fight for justice. We can usually root for superheroes, because in the end they are going to save the day.

But with Tony Stark, also known as Iron Man, the lines are blurred. Tony Stark is a flawed human being, that's for sure. When he dons his Iron Man armor, he doesn't quite overcome his human faults. He doesn't always get right from wrong. He is phenomenally wealthy, but sometimes he exploits those who aren't as fortunate. He has developed amazingly powerful weapons and armor, but he doesn't always use those to fight for the purest of social causes. In some ways, Tony Stark and Iron Man give us negative examples of what it means to be a hero.

This chapter focuses on the division between "haves" and "have-nots" in our society. What is a hero to do?

Jesus' ministry reached out to the rich and poor alike, but he vowed that those categories would be turned on their heads in the kingdom of God. When Jesus turned over the money changers' tables in the Temple, he also disrupted our ideas about the importance of money in our lives. The existence of the haves and the have-nots in our world is a great theological question that is yet to be answered. Even our superheroes sometimes miss the mark, but the ministry of Jesus challenges us to look for a future where equality reigns.

A HAPPY MONK IS THE ONE WITH THE KEYS

"If you wish to be perfect, go, sell your possessions, and give the money to the poor, and you will have treasure in heaven; then come, follow me."

Matthew 19:21

Some places just look like the kingdom of God to me.

The local homeless shelter in my town reveals the Kingdom, because it is a place where people who have lost everything are offered a new start. Our confirmation class at church also reveals the Kingdom; as students grasp a profound new truth, I think of the crowd hearing Jesus' parables for the first time. The kingdom of God is a place where the line between haves and have-nots is blurred, nonsensical, and unfixed. At different times Jesus says the kingdom of God is like a mustard seed, a pearl, and a treasure, all of which are small but great, buried but revealed. What does the kingdom of God look like to you?

Several years ago I had the great fortune to visit a monastery right in my own backyard, in Saint Benedict, Louisiana. St. Joseph Abbey, founded in 1889, is a sanctuary of prayer and work for the Benedictine monks who live there. Every year, those seeking ordination in the Louisiana Conference of The United Methodist Church spend several days with the brothers to meditate on the calling of vocational ministry. Benedictine monks make three vows when they enter the monastic life: obedience, stability, and conversion of life. They do not make a vow of poverty. Instead, the brothers hold everything in common. As one of the brothers shared with me, "A happy monk is the one with the keys."

Holding everything in common sounds like it might be easy in such a setting, surrounded by people who spend their days in a secluded area, praying and working. But this is not the case. For example, if a disagreement escalates dramatically, the vow of stability means that leaving is not an option. Monks are called to live and stay in a particular place. They are not to avoid, escape, or ignore one another. Forgiveness takes on a whole new meaning when there is nowhere to go.

What would it look like for you to share all your possessions with those in need? One day a rich young man came to Jesus and asked what he needed to do beyond keeping the commandments. Jesus responded, "If you wish to be perfect, go, sell your possessions, and give the money to the poor, and you will have treasure in heaven; then come, follow me" (Matthew 19:21). This is one of Jesus' most difficult teachings. Sell all my possessions? Give the money to the poor? Maybe the toughest instruction is the last one: follow me.

Jesus invites us into a new life where worth doesn't rely on money or possessions.

Jesus' words to the rich young man certainly were about money, but they were about much more also. For many of us, we could sell everything we own today, and the next paycheck would be just two weeks away. Maybe the story is about offering God what costs you everything, or at least what we think is everything.

The kingdom of God is a topsy-turvy world in which the relationship between haves and have-nots is turned upside down. Listen to Jesus' words to the crowd in Luke's Gospel:

> *"Blessed are you who are poor,*
> *for yours is the kingdom of God.*
> *"Blessed are you who are hungry now,*
> *for you will be filled. . . .*
> *"But woe to you who are rich,*
> *for you have received your consolation.*
> *"Woe to you who are full now,*
> *for you will be hungry."*
> *Luke 6:20-21, 24-25*

On the surface this seems like a simple economic role reversal, but this doesn't further the Kingdom. Reversing roles only creates another power imbalance. Jesus has something more liberating in mind.

A clue is found in Luke's Gospel in an occurrence following Christ's resurrection. The resurrected Lord appears before the disciples, showing them his scarred hands and feet. Then he asks for something to eat. The disciples offer him broiled fish. He takes it and eats it in their presence (Luke 24:36-43).

This act of eating is a symbol of God's kingdom, where the hungry are filled and those who are filled, feed. The Resurrection is the affirmation that God's kingdom is coming to fruition, and it is a life in which the division between have and have-not disappears by the power of grace.

A monk who has the keys is certainly a happy monk, but that happiness turns to joy when he, and all of us, can offer that key to another soul.

Do you think Jesus was truly preaching about "have" and "have-not," or was he trying to show us that there is no such thing?

How do you think Jesus would define poverty? Would he say it was a good thing or a bad thing?

If you had been the rich young man who approached Jesus, how would you have responded to Jesus' words?

SUPERHEROES

Iron Man[1]

Comic

Publisher: Marvel Comics
Created by: Stan Lee, Larry Lieber, Don Heck, and Jack Kirby
First appeared: *Tales of Suspense #39*, March 1963

Character

Alter Ego: Anthony Edward "Tony" Stark
Species: Human
Hometown: New York, New York
Team Affiliations: Avengers, S.H.I.E.L.D.
Powers:
Genius-level intellect
Superhuman strength
Supersonic flight
Enemies:
The Mandarin
Iron Monger
Crimson Dynamo

Interesting fact

Forbes magazine named Tony Stark in their article ranking
the wealthiest fictional characters.[2]

SUPERHEROES

Origin

When wealthy weapons-inventor Tony Stark is captured by terrorists, he is grievously wounded by shrapnel from an explosive. Thanks to the help of a fellow captive, Tony is able to survive. The terrorists expect Tony to build weapons for them, but Tony is able to escape with an armored suit made from the provided parts. When he returns home from captivity, he rededicates his life and business to making things that will benefit people rather than making weapons. He also continues to develop his armored suit invention, wearing it to act as Iron Man and help people directly.

Heroic moment

In the acclaimed comic book series dubbed "Demon in a Bottle," Tony Stark, the alter ego of Iron Man, confronts his alcoholism. One night in a drunken rage, Tony yells at his butler, who immediately resigns. With the help of a friend, Tony decides to get sober once and for all. He works through withdrawal and addiction, apologizes to his butler, and moves forward into a life without alcohol.[3]

A VISION OF A KINGDOM

*I can do all things through him who
strengthens me.*

Philippians 4:13

Ultimately it is power that divides the haves from the have-nots. Whether the source of this power is money, influence, or culture, power is what divides us. In Philippians 4, Paul writes about being on both sides of the power divide: "I know what it is to have little, and I know what it is to have plenty. In any and all circumstances I have learned the secret of being well-fed and of going hungry, of having plenty and of being in need. I can do all things through him who strengthens me" (Philippians 4:12-13). What "all things" is Paul talking about? Does he really mean "all," and if so, how is it that Christ strengthens us?

I keep a picture on my desk of Walt Disney surveying the undeveloped land that was soon to be Walt Disney World. Walt Disney is one of my heroes because of his vision and his ability to tell a good story. I keep this picture on my desk because it represents one of the ways I understand the church. One of the roles of the church is to build the kingdom of God, or to look at undeveloped land and see a kingdom.

Walt Disney finally decided on the property in central Florida because his imagination appeared to be limitless. "There's enough land here to hold all the ideas and plans we can possibly imagine," he declared.[4] It takes incredible vision and faith in your calling to purchase 27,443 acres of land for plans that weren't even on the drawing board. Walt Disney never shied away from the seemingly impossible.

One of my congregation's favorite verses is "I can do all things through [Christ] who strengthens me." It's a verse of encouragement and hope. Paul is writing to the church in Philippi, which has supported him throughout his ministry, and he is thanking them for their continued work in the Kingdom. When Paul says, "I can do all things," he isn't necessarily talking about developing 27,000 acres of land into a theme park, or climbing Mount Everest, or going to the moon; rather, he is saying that no matter what life offers, he is choosing to remain connected to Christ. No matter what I do, he seems to say, I can do it through Christ.

Because I am a United Methodist pastor, our family has moved quite often. Every time we move, our family sits down and goes through our things to decide what we need, what we want, and what we would like to give or throw away. Moving forces you to have a discussion about what really matters. Paul can endure all things because, through his connection with Christ, he knows what really matters in life. He can endure being in need. He can endure having plenty. He can endure the bad times. He can endure the good times. He has learned the secret to being content in any and every circumstance. Living a life in Christ doesn't mean you are now good at everything; rather, it means that you begin to truly discover what God is calling you to.

Several years ago, a friend of mine was sitting at home during the holiday season lamenting the fact that her husband was overseas. She sent him a Christmas card so that he could have a little slice of home while fighting in Afghanistan. When he received the card, he sent a letter home saying that the other troops were jealous because he was the only one who opened a Christmas card. That gave her an idea. After she prayed about it for a while, she brought the idea to her church asking, "Do you think we could collect holiday cards for our troops overseas?" The first year they collected 1,200. The next year they collected 12,000, then 35,000 then 48,000. If I asked you to collect 48,000 holiday cards for troops, it might sound impossible, but it's not. It started with one person meeting a need by sending one card and praying about what to do next. "I can do all things" doesn't mean that if we pray hard enough we can fly or shoot laser beams out of our eyes or run faster than a speeding bullet. It means we can do what God is calling us to do, no matter how difficult the task, no matter how long it takes, no matter how much fun we are going to have.

When we are connected to Christ, our vision begins to change. Saul was traveling the road to Damascus, and a great light blinded him. He heard from the heavens, "Saul, Saul, why do you persecute me?" (Acts 9:4). He remained blind for three days. Then Ananias, the real hero of the story, visited with Saul. Even though Ananias was a Christian visiting the great persecutor of the church, Ananias healed him. Scripture says that something like scales fell from Paul's eyes, and he could once again see. When Christ offers something new, when Christ offers you purpose, your vision begins to change. You begin to see the world differently.

Vision matters. What you see matters. Look around in your mind's eye. What do you see? Do you see friends and family? Do you see the body of Christ? Do you see that person you've been meaning to forgive, but just needed a sign from God to do it? Do you see a revolution? Do you see the world being turned upside down for all the right reasons? When we look in each other's eyes, do you see the face of Christ looking back? Who is missing from the faces you see? Are the faces white, black, rich, poor, gay, or straight? The "all things" to which Paul refers begins with us and the vision we see of God's kingdom. What kind of vision have your heroes cast?

What are some similarities between Walt Disney's vision of the world and Jesus' vision of the world? some differences?

What are some ways you could help others outside your church during this Lent and Easter season? What's one step you could take to start?

If you close your eyes and envision the body of Christ, what do you see?

LONELY TOGETHER

It is not good that the man should be alone.
Genesis 2:18

Last year, I took my daughters to see the movie *Coraline*.[5] Coraline, the main character, is a different kind of hero. She is a young girl who discovers an alternate world in which her parents are kind, only her favorite foods are served, and there's always time to play. All she has to do to live in this world is to sew buttons in place of her eyes. At first it seems to be an easy trade, but soon she discovers that this alternate world is built on lies. Coraline realizes that even if the real world is difficult, truth is more valuable than fantasy.

Sometimes I fear that our love of technology has become like giving up our eyes for a pair of buttons. Several years ago, I helped lead a prayer service at the Goodson Chapel at Duke Divinity School. In order to get to the service I had to take the East Campus bus over to West Campus. When I got onto the bus, it was standing room only. Everyone was so immersed in their phones that it was difficult even to ask people to make room. After the bus emptied out, I ran over to get ready for the service. The chapel soon filled with many of the students I had just seen on the bus, and I was thankful to see so many new faces. Near the end of the service I had the opportunity to hear prayer concerns from the students after they came up to receive Communion. I was shocked by the frequency of one particular concern.

I had thought students would seek prayer for their grades, relationships, or finances, but when I heard person after person say, "I am so lonely," I was heartbroken and confused. I was heartbroken because loneliness was never God's plan for us. When God created the heavens and the earth, God looked upon the creation and said that it was good. Scripture emphasizes the goodness of what God was doing over and over again, which is why it is so striking when God said, "It is not good that the man should be alone" (Genesis 2:18). This is the first time that something in creation is "not good," and it never is good for human beings to be alone.

Humanity was created to be together. On the one hand, technology makes it easier to connect with one another. In an instant I can text, tweet, and chat with someone without having to carve out time for travel, coffee, or mailing a letter. On the other hand, instantaneous communication sometimes means we leave little room for thinking about what we are saying. Using our thumbs to communicate offers an unhelpful degree of separation.

It gives us just enough separation to offer unfiltered thoughts, but we forget that the other person can hear everything.

How can you be lonely on an overcrowded bus? When everyone is immersed in what's going on, on his or her phone, it's hard to see the community God has surrounded you with. Let's think about our hands for a moment. What you do with your hands is a great way to think about how you connect with the people around you. What do you hold in your hands most often each day? Maybe it's the steering wheel of your car because you are commuting to work, sitting in the car pool line, or maybe a friend or family member is sick and you're going back and forth from home to hospital. Maybe your computer keys are touching your fingertips most often because of the invoices you organize or e-mails you write. Maybe your cell phone monopolizes your hands because you are connecting with people or scrolling through Instagram for funny cat pictures. But how often are our hands folded in prayer or unoccupied in order to receive what God has in mind? If we primarily connect with one another as we are hunched over a hand-held screen, we get an idea of how St. Augustine described sin as an inwardly turned soul.

Sometimes life offers unintended consequences. Think about Prohibition in the 1920s. The Eighteenth Amendment was successful in keeping local distilleries and bars from selling alcohol, but it gave rise to organized crime. Consider the consequences of introducing kudzu, which is an ornamental plant introduced to the United States in 1876; but it grew so quickly in the American South that it drove out many native plants. And I recently laughed out loud at a text I received with a picture of bored people at a church committee meeting. Under the graphic of drowsy participants was the caption "An unintended consequence of the Resurrection." I will admit that I love thinking about the relationship between God and innovative technology, but one of the unintended consequences of technology is the increasing gap between have and have-not. Steve Jobs is a hero of innovation, transforming the way we connect with one another. One of the unintended consequences of that connectivity is that those who have access to new technology begin to forget that not everyone has the same access.

In my local church we are thinking about investing in a mobile app to keep our members connected with announcements, online giving, and geolocation technology. It's really exciting, but I am thankful that someone asked how we would continue to connect with people who did not have access to a smartphone. An unintended consequence of new technology is how quick we are to make some feel they are on the outside looking in.

Those in marketing know how to use to their advantage the desire to be on the inside. We want to be welcomed, we want to fit in, and we want to have a sense of community. From slacks and loafers to wallet chains and leather jackets, every community has immediate and clear indicators of who is welcome. The welcome sign is not so apparent with technology. Phones buzz in purses, Facebook pages have logins, and Snapchat is temporary. In other words, it's easy to be exclusive because the language is a private discourse.

It's difficult to share the gospel if your language is exclusively private; and the more we digitize our connection with one another, the stronger the temptation to be exclusive becomes. Could it be that the current division in our politics and churches is an unintended consequence of technology? As much as I love technology, sometimes I feel that, a bit like our hero Coraline, I'm trading my eyes for the newest iPhone. Maybe it's time to look up and see God's goodness.

> O taste and see that the LORD is good;
> happy are those who take refuge in him.
>
> *Psalm 34:8*

What are some ways in which technology connects you to other people? What are some ways it separates you?

Think of a time when you felt most alone. How did it feel? What caused it? What did you do in response?

What are some ways in which your hunger for community helps you? What are some ways it hurts you?

REAL-LIFE HEROES

Saint Teresa of Calcutta[6]

Born Anjezë Gonxhe Bojaxhiu in Macedonia in 1910, Saint Teresa of Calcutta, popularly known as Mother Teresa, was an Albanian-Indian nun who dedicated her life to serving the poor in Calcutta, India. Saint Teresa entered the convent when she was eighteen years old, serving first as a high-school teacher for girls in Darjeeling, India, where she was struck by the intense poverty and suffering around her. One day while riding a train, she felt "a call within a call" that she was to "follow Christ into the slums to serve him among the poorest of the poor." After training as a nurse, she moved to the slums of Calcutta and began visiting and caring for the sick and impoverished people around her. Soon many volunteers joined her, forming the Missionaries of Charity. Saint Teresa was awarded the Nobel Peace Prize in 1979. She died in 1997, was beatified in 2003, and was canonized a saint by Pope Francis in 2016.

I see God in every human being. When I wash the leper's wounds I feel I am nursing the Lord himself. Is it not a beautiful experience?[7]

BLESSINGS AND THANKSGIVINGS

From his fullness we have all received, grace
upon grace.

John 1:16

There are four ways in which we share information with each other, and when there is an imbalance of power, the way we tell our stories is important. Imagine that your leadership has decided to change the color of the sanctuary carpet to green, and they've called a meeting to get feedback on the decision. First, there is the *public* discourse, which is out in the open for all to hear. In the public there is an unspoken order in which we all play a part. Someone gets up and talks about how green is the color of growth, it represents life, and because most of the liturgical year falls in common time and the liturgical color of common time is green, we would save money on worship visuals. Someone else gets up in opposition to what was said, saying that green is trendy and will be soon out of date, and frankly, green carpet is hideous.

Then the community takes a break and there is great chatter in the hallways. This kind of language is a *private* discourse. This communication is not intended for the general public to hear. Think of the poor soul who forgot his microphone was on when the cameras stopped rolling, or the conversations in the hallways after a church meeting. These conversations are meant for insiders, which, when offered in the public arena, either make us laugh like watching a newscaster chat with a coworker when they don't know they are live, or can make us cringe when someone says what they really think about someone. This is when you gather with your friends to say what you really want to say about the green carpet without a threat of judgment.

You gather back together to talk about the carpet and someone gets up to tell a story about green, without actually using the word *green*. This language is *disguised*. They stand in the middle of the room telling a story about a bullfrog in Ireland standing in the clover and what a beautiful picture it is. They will neither say if they are in favor or if they hate the green carpet, but it's pretty clear where they stand. Many of Jesus' parables follow this pattern of disguise. For example, the story of the good Samaritan was certainly about being a neighbor, but it was also a commentary on the division between Jews and Samaritans.

Then there is *defiant* language, which is also in the public arena, but the unspoken roles and rules are broken and the language is no longer safe. "I hate this idea, and if the carpet is green we are leaving the church." It's like when Jesus said to the Pharisees, "Woe to you, scribes and Pharisees, hypocrites! For you are like whitewashed tombs" (Matthew 23:27a). Understanding how language is being used might help us understand Jesus' Kingdom language and what it might mean. Understanding how we use language can also help us be aware of ways we unintentionally make people feel as though they are on the outside, or on the other side of God's favor.

The division between haves and have-nots can sometimes unfairly be seen as a sign of God's blessing or lack thereof. When my wife and I started having children, we were quick to say that we were "blessed." But how do people without children understand this language of blessing?

One night we were out to dinner with some friends who were finding it difficult to have children of their own. Seeing their despair and sadness made us realize that we needed to change our language.

Instead of saying that we were blessed to have children, we began saying that we were thankful for having a family with little ones. Changing our language from blessing to thankfulness is one of the ways we can dissolve the divide between us and our friends.

Changing the way we think about God's Word and world can be scary, which is why Jesus so often said, "Peace be with you." One of my heroes, Dr. Martin Luther King Jr., knew the fear of uncertainty and the fear of change. In his sermon "A Knock at Midnight," King acknowledged the darkness but said that we "can walk through the dark night with the radiant conviction that all things work together for good for those who love God. Even the most starless midnight may herald the dawn of some great fulfillment."[8]

When you start to break down the dividing line between have and have-not, things can look chaotic and uncertain. There was a church that wanted to expand their food pantry ministry outside the walls of the church to the local men's shelter. Their outreach was going really well, and trust began to grow between the men at the shelter and the servants at the church. Many of the servants began inviting the men to join them for worship on Sunday mornings.

Several weeks went by, and the church members were wondering why they weren't seeing any of their friends from the shelter at worship. After asking around, one of the men from the shelter had the courage to say, "I visited a few times, but when I arrived, the folks at the door pointed me to the food pantry instead of the sanctuary. After a while, I gave up." There's no question that the church was doing great work in the community, but pointing some to the sanctuary and others to the food pantry reveals a stigma, fear, and cultural assumption that hadn't yet been completely overcome.

Changing our language from blessing to thanksgiving helps us change our understanding of how God is working in the world.

It's not that the church was blessed and the men from the shelter were not blessed; rather, the church could give thanks for the opportunity to share the gospel, and the shelter could give thanks for the opportunity to receive.

In any given situation, you are either a candidate for a miracle or the channel through which the miracle happens. In other words, blessings take many forms. It is a blessing to give, and it is a blessing to receive. Giving thanks for God's grace that brings the two together helps us see an even deeper meaning to Paul's words: "I know what it is to have little, and I know what it is to have plenty. In any and all circumstances I have learned the secret of being well-fed and of going hungry, of having plenty and of being in need. I can do all things through him who strengthens me" (Philippians 4:12-13).

The kingdom of God is a place where have and have-not get turned upside down. Unlike the world of Tony Stark, the poor are blessed because the wealthy share. The mournful are comforted, and those with comfort offer lament. Sometimes it appears that some are blessed and others are not, but in God's kingdom our thankfulness for what Christ is doing reveals that all are blessed when we invite Christ to be the center of our life. God isn't a Robin Hood who steals from the wealthy and gives to the poor, because it's not only money God is calling us to share. God is calling us to share our very self with one another and the world. Iron Man puts on an amazing suit built from his vast resources to fight for the little guy. It's a suit built on the side of the have for the have-not. God did things a bit differently. Instead of putting on an amazing suit, Jesus emptied himself and put on humanity. Jesus was fully divine in majesty and glory, but also fully human, meaning it was a glory that experienced suffering, hunger, and pain. Jesus was born, literally in the lowest place on earth to reveal that God's glory knows no bounds. In Jesus, haves and have-nots come together to reveal a Kingdom of abundant and everlasting love. There is have, there is have-not, and there is the kingdom of God in which the difference between the two is buried under the weight of a cross.

Give examples from your own life of public discourse, private discourse, disguised language, and defiant language.

Of the four kinds of discourse described above, give an example of a way in which that discourse can be used positively.

Of the four kinds of discourse described above, give an example of a way in which that discourse can be used negatively.

Chapter Five

OLD, NEW, AND COVENANT

In the beginning, Captain America was just Steve Rogers, a skinny kid from 1940s New York who was transformed into a super-soldier by the government. Many years later, Iron Man, Thor, Giant-Man, and Wasp found Rogers frozen in a block of ice, preserved by the super-soldier serum in his body.

Since then, as a member of the Avengers group of superheroes, Captain America has been fighting crime and righting wrongs, but not without the struggles of being suddenly reincarnated in a totally new and different reality. Most notably, Captain America has old-fashioned values (formed during the Depression era and World War II) that laid the foundation for his careful code of ethics and strong sense of leadership. Captain America's "old" moral code ends up serving him well in the modern world, but other nuances of contemporary culture (a woman for a doctor??) are sometimes lost on him.

SETTING THE SCENE

Then a voice came from heaven, "I have
glorified [my name], and I will glorify it again."
The crowd standing there heard it and said that it
was thunder.

John 12:28-29

"Out with the old and in with the new" as a motto for change is a bit misleading. With radical change, the old aren't being valued and the new have no history. Think about your church youth group. Every year there is a new class of students who bring their own unique gifts, but the seniors in the group know the traditions and the unspoken rules of Sunday night fellowship. Every year there is a delicate dance between new ideas and trusted traditions. The same is true for growing churches. Having lots of new faces is great, but it can also be a problem. How do you incorporate the fire and energy of new disciples into trusted, valued traditions?

Pentecost offers a great model to follow:

All of them were filled with the Holy Spirit
and began to speak in other languages, as the
Spirit gave them ability.

Now there were devout Jews from every nation
under heaven living in Jerusalem. And at this
sound the crowd gathered and was bewildered,
because each one heard them speaking in the
native language of each.

Acts 2:4-6

This passage offers us a picture of the relationship between the old and the new. Pouring out the Holy Spirit upon the disciples was a radical shift in the way God communed with us (including the excitement of something new), but those gathered together heard their own language being spoken (such as the comfort of something old).

I once served a church that gave me two rules to follow. First, they didn't want the pastor to wear a tie on Sundays. That was easy! Second, they didn't want anything traditional in their worship service. This was a challenge I was willing to accept. After a few Sundays with my new congregation, I chose as the opening hymn "Victory in Jesus." It was a risk because it doesn't get more traditional than this 1939 hymn by Eugene M. Bartlett. But what if we played it in the style of Creedence Clearwater Revival's "Born on the Bayou"?

It became one of the congregation's favorite songs. It worked because the music fit their culture well (we were in south Louisiana, after all), but the melody and words were unchanged. One worshiper caught me after the service and said, "You're offering them tradition, and they don't even know it." Bingo! It was change that honored the old and incorporated the new. Successful change means listening to years of wisdom while capturing the passion of new ideas.

Once you know the rules, you can begin to bend them carefully. Consider Mozart's composition "Twelve Variations on 'Ah! vous dirai-je, maman' (more commonly known as "Twinkle, Twinkle, Little Star"). At the beginning of Mozart's variations on the familiar nursery rhyme, you hear the famous tune, establishing the rules of the melody. Then the notes around the melody ornament the main theme. Next, the melody is played in the lower notes with the higher notes doing something completely different. Sometimes the music is soft and the notes are long; other times the music is loud and quickly played. About halfway through the piece, the theme is played in a minor key, which really changes the piece's feel. I wonder how different the melody would have become if Mozart had kept going to fourteen, twenty, or forty variations. Would we even recognize the original melody by the time we arrived at the fortieth variation?

Now imagine going from Mozart's first variation immediately to his twelfth variation. The piece would be jarring, uninteresting, and misunderstood. It would sound like two different, unrelated songs. That's the beauty of the theme and variation. It's not so much about the destination; rather, it's about the musical journey.

Similarly, without journeying through all of God's story in Scripture, Jesus makes little sense. Jesus isn't so much an innovator as one who remembers God's story and fulfills it. In John's Gospel the disciples heard a voice from heaven proclaim, "I have glorified it, and I will glorify it again" (John 12:28). Some heard it as nonsensical thunder, but Jesus revealed that it was God's voice foreshadowing Jesus' own death. The crowd said in reply, "We have heard from the law that the Messiah remains forever. How can you say the Son of Man will be lifted up?" (v. 34). The crowd was stuck in the first variation. From their point of view, Jesus appeared to be a haphazard rule-breaker, when in actuality his healings, teachings, miracles, mission, and suffering were the fulfillment of God's story, bridging creation with resurrection.

Describe a time in your own life when you had to balance the old and the new. How did you attempt that balance, and how successful were you?

Give your response to this statement: "Jesus isn't so much an innovator as one who remembers God's story and fulfills it."

To what degree do you think it's true that we must journey through all of God's Scripture for Jesus to make sense?

SUPERHEROES

Captain America[1]

Comic

Publisher: Marvel Comics
Created by: Joe Simon and Jack Kirby
First appeared: *Captain America Comics* #1, March 1941

Character

Alter ego: Steve Rogers
Species: Human
Team affiliations: Avengers, S.H.I.E.L.D.
Powers:
Peak physical condition
Expert hand-to-hand and armed combatant
Expert with tactics and strategy
Equipment:
Nearly indestructible vibranium shield.
Enemies:
Red Skull
Baron Zemo
Hydra

Interesting fact

When he was created in 1940, his name was almost Super American.

SUPERHEROES

Origin

Steve Rogers wanted to join the army during World War II, but was rejected due to his weak physical condition. However, he was accepted into a top secret program that managed to transform him into the pinnacle of physical perfection. With his new abilities, Steve served the army as Captain America, fighting against enemies that ordinary soldiers wouldn't be able to face.

During one mission, Steve is thrown from a plane into freezing cold waters. Frozen solid, he is able to survive thanks to his heightened endurance. Several decades later, he is found and revived by the Avengers, whom he quickly joins. Steve continues to fight for his country and his beliefs as Captain America, even though the world has changed from what he once knew.

Heroic moment

When Steve Rogers, Captain America's alter ego, is training to be a soldier in World War II, his commander tosses a grenade into a group of recruits. Instead of scattering like everyone else, Steve throws himself on the grenade. This is a preview of Captain America's constant willingness to sacrifice himself for the well-being of others.[2]

HOW TO INTRODUCE A HERO

In the beginning was the Word, and the Word was with God, and the Word was God.

John 1:1

Have you ever been in a situation where you wanted to do something new but heard the dreaded "But we've always done it this way"? Whenever comic book sales are slumping, publishers will often reboot or restart a character's story. Sometimes it's exciting to reboot a character with a new origin story, and sometimes it doesn't work.

Batman's 2016 reboot in DC Comics "New 52" series was thrilling, interesting, and fit well with the established story. Bruce Wayne returned to the role of Batman, the character got younger (he had been Batman for a only few years), and he was given a new cast of allies. That reboot was exciting and successful.

But then you have Marvel's debacle with Captain America's history. Fans were not pleased when it was revealed that the Cap had been an agent of the evil Hydra all along. It added a new layer to Captain America's history, but not a welcome one. Many fans hope the storyline goes away somehow. Maybe it was all a dream?

Introducing something new can be tricky. A pastor told me that early in his ministry, he had tried to introduce a new way of celebrating Holy Communion to his community. He started having weekly Communion in a congregation that normally celebrated Communion once a month. He didn't ask anyone's permission, send out a survey, or explain why the change had happened. The congregation reacted strongly. Some protested, "But you are such a good preacher, we want to make sure you have enough time to offer the Word every week!" Others complained, "It's not special if we do it every week." Still others said simply, "It just takes too long." So, they went back to monthly Communion.

A few years later the pastor tried a second approach. He went to the leadership team and said, "During the six weeks of Lent I would like to try weekly Communion, and then after Easter we will go back to the normal schedule." The six weeks of Lent came and went without any pushback. On Easter Sunday they celebrated Communion, and the following week was the first Sunday of the month, so they were expecting Communion anyway. After serving weekly communion for eight weeks straight, the pastor thought he was in the clear, until he heard one of the leaders say, "Finally, next Sunday we will be back to the normal routine." So, they went back to monthly Communion. Again.

Finally the pastor tried a third approach: honesty. (What a radical idea!) He gathered the worship team and simply told them how important weekly Communion can be to the worshiping community. They had an honest conversation about length, meaning, and flow of worship. After spending time in prayer, the team decided to give it a shot. Not everyone was happy with the change, but all were on the same page as to why the change happened.

When something new is introduced to a community, the way it's announced is crucial. A good example is the Gospels of Mark and Luke. Each Gospel introduces Jesus in a different way.

In the Gospel of Mark, Jesus seems to appear out of nowhere. There is little background offered, no birth narrative, and the opening verse doesn't even include a verb: "The beginning of the good news of Jesus Christ, the Son of God" (Mark 1:1). But that incomplete sentence offers a radical insight into what Mark finds important, in his words *The beginning*. Mark doesn't hold a high regard for what went on before the beginning of Jesus' ministry. We don't hear anything about Mary or Joseph or a miraculous birth. Mark is not concerned with having all the answers or impressive multi-syllabic theological terms. Mark wants you to jump on board his passionate, fast-moving train of good news.

Luke's Gospel, in contrast, offers "an orderly account" (Luke 1:1) of what has been written and said about Christ. We see shepherds and angels and a manger. We hear the stories of the good Samaritan and the prodigal son and the lost sheep. Luke takes this approach because he wants you to share the gospel. His orderly account is a colorful and memorable one. Luke wants us to know that what God is doing is miraculous, powerful, and subversive. In a way, Luke's Gospel is like the *Schoolhouse Rock* of Gospels. If you want to teach someone how to use a conjunction, playing "Conjunction Junction" is always the way to go! Luke wants you to remember the gospel, and to know that the gospel is for those on the margins of society, so for those who have been marginalized, this Gospel is living water.

And then there's John's Gospel. It is altogether different. In Mark, Jesus appears out of nowhere. Matthew lengthens the story to show that Jesus is a descendant of Abraham. Luke extends the story further, bringing Jesus' lineage all the way to Adam and Eve. John outdoes them all saying, "In the beginning was the Word, and the Word was with God, and the Word was God" (John 1:1). Each Gospel offers a different understanding of when Jesus' story begins, when this new movement of the good news began, which means that new is not something you can put on a calendar or take out of a box. Being made new is something Christ alone offers. It's not throwing away the old, but understanding it in a new way.

If you set out to introduce Jesus, how would your story begin?

What advice would you give someone who is hoping to start something new in a community or group?

Think of times in your own life when you tried something new and it failed. Think of times when it succeeded. What do you think was the difference?

How do you explain differences among the four Gospels? What are the benefits of having differing accounts of Jesus' life and ministry?

ORIGINS MATTER

Truly this man was God's Son!
Matthew 27:54

The world is changing so quickly. In her ninety years, my grandmother has seen everything from horse-drawn carriages to self-driving cars, from one television for the whole neighborhood to YouTube on every smartphone, from a telephone party line to Facetime. With change happening so rapidly, sometimes it's hard for one generation to talk with the next. Baby Boomers don't understand Generation X, and Millennials are beginning to lose ground to Generation OMG. Phrases such as "You're too entitled" and "You're too institutional" suggest that one generation has nothing to do with the other. Maybe this is why Matthew begins his Gospel detailing the generations that gave birth to Jesus.

A genealogy can reveal a great deal about a person's identity. Matthew wants us to know where Jesus came from, not only so we know that Jesus was real and walked the earth, but so we know that God has been working on salvation for a long, long time.

Matthew divides Jesus' genealogy into three sections. The first section is a story of great victory. It begins with faithful Abraham and ends with King David, who united Israel under one flag and laid the political foundation for the first temple in Jerusalem.

The second section is a story of embarrassing defeat, ending with King Jechoniah in exile. Remembering the Exile reminds us that Jesus is related to some flawed people: Jacob the scoundrel, Tamar the prostitute, Ahaziah the murderer.

But the story doesn't end in defeat. The third section leads up to the birth of Jesus, which ultimately becomes a story of salvation. In that story, God puts on flesh, the flesh of kings and scoundrels, walks among us to show us how to live, dies on a cross to show us how to die, and lives again to show us that this story of victory and defeat, which we call life, ends in resurrection.

Whereas Mark tells us from the beginning that Jesus is the Son of God, Matthew makes us earn it. First Jesus is the son of David and the son of Abraham, which means that Jesus is a king who will suffer. This bulleted story of victory, defeat, and salvation prepares us for what is said at the foot of the cross:

> *Now when the centurion and those with him, who were keeping watch over Jesus, saw the earthquake and what took place [on the cross], they were terrified and said, "Truly this man was God's Son!"*
>
> *Matthew 27:54*

Organizations have genealogies too. When we enter the church, we inherit a tradition, a DNA, that's thousands of years old. But the way that DNA is communicated depends on the behavior of the community. How are we offering Christ? What are we saying about Christ when we serve? What are we saying about Christ when we don't serve? Who would Christ welcome in this place, and not just welcome but invite and seek and serve?

"An account of the genealogy of Jesus, the Messiah, the son of David, the son of Abraham" (Matthew 1:1). It is a family history of victory, defeat, and ultimately, salvation. Through his life, death, and resurrection, Christ offers a salvation stronger than the blood that runs through our own veins. It is radical acceptance of both kings and scoundrels, and it is a call to action to do the will of God so that this generation and generations to come will know and live the good news of God's love.

People of my generation have seen more profound changes than any other generation in history. Do you agree or disagree, and why?

What are some advantages and disadvantages of starting an account of Jesus' life with a genealogy?

What is your church's genealogy? How is its "DNA" passed down to new members?

THE BRUSHSTROKES OF
GOD'S MASTERPIECE

For by your words you will be justified, and by your words you will be condemned.

Matthew 12:37

Each time our Gospel writers put pen to parchment, they offer more about Jesus' origin. As we've seen, Mark doesn't say much about where Jesus came from; Jesus rather abruptly appears on the scene. Matthew tells us a bit more, saying that Jesus is the Son of David and Son of Abraham. Luke goes back even further, beginning his genealogy not with Abraham but with Adam.

The Fourth Gospel, John, trumps them all. John starts with, "In the beginning was the Word, and the Word was with God, and the Word was God" (John 1:1). Not only does John reach back to the beginning of time; he also offers more on Jesus' identity.

John wants us to think about Creation itself. God created through words. Words are important. Words are valuable. Words make ideas real.

We often first get to know people through words. We learn their name, where they are from, what they value, and what they don't. John wants us to know that Jesus is the Word of God made flesh, the Word revealing the full and true nature of God, which is why he brings us back to Creation: in the beginning. This Word of God is not something new. It was here all along. What we see in Jesus is a picture of who God is.

Words are like brushstrokes. If you get too close to a painting, the brushstrokes mean little. But take a step back and consider the brushstrokes together; they reveal something greater than themselves. Similarly, words point to a truth beyond themselves. Jesus' life, suffering, death, and resurrection are the brushstrokes of God's masterpiece.

But our identity is created by more than words. Words are only as powerful as the fruitfulness of our actions. Jesus offers a story about the relationship between words and actions:

> "A man had two sons; he went to the first and
> said, 'Son, go and work in the vineyard today.'
> He answered, 'I will not'; but later he changed his
> mind and went. The father went to the second and
> said the same; and he answered, 'I go, sir'; but he
> did not go. Which of the two did the will of his
> father?"
>
> *Matthew 21:28-31*

Jesus goes on to say that the first son is the one who will enter the kingdom of heaven. We do not earn our salvation, but our actions reveal the fruitfulness of our faith. If our words aren't backed up by our actions, it doesn't take long for the words to become empty and meaningless. It's hard to trust someone who says one thing and does another. John wants us to recognize that Jesus is God's Word, and God's Word can be trusted.

Our heroes are people of words and action. Simply put, they do what they say, and they speak truth into what they do. Malala Yousafzai is a champion for women's education in her native Pakistan and around the world. In October 2012, a Taliban gunman attempted to murder her for zealously promoting education for girls. He approached a bus of students and shouted, "Which one of you is Malala?" Instead of shying away, she stood firm, identified herself, and was shot in the head, which nearly ended her life. But Malala recovered and continued her work to promote education for girls. In July 2013, she addressed the United Nations, saying,

> The terrorists thought they would change my aims and stop my ambitions, but nothing changed in my life except this: weakness, fear and hopelessness died. Strength, power and courage was born.[3]

Malala is an amazing example of the power of words and of having the courage to stand by them.

Words and actions offer us a good picture of who someone is, which is why the Gospels are so important. Jesus, as God's Word, empowered by the Holy Spirit, offers us a picture of who God is. Jesus' teachings are the brushstrokes, his healings are the colors, and his death and resurrection help us make sense of it all.

Each Gospel builds on the others to stretch and bend the frame, filling in God's picture of salvation. Four Gospels—Matthew, Mark, Luke, and John—along with a fifth. Sometimes that fifth Gospel is hard to find. It is often hidden but easily shared, difficult to understand but simply known. The fifth Gospel is the story you tell through your words and actions. What is the story you might tell about how Christ is offering salvation in you?

Which version of Jesus' origin as told in the Gospels do you like best? Why?

What are some ways in which Jesus can be communicated through words or as Word? What are some ways in which that metaphor falls short?

What's an example of a time when you produced words but no corresponding action? a time when your words and actions matched up?

REAL-LIFE HEROES

Mikaila Ulmer[4]

When Mikaila Ulmer was four years old, she got stung by two bees in one week. Her mother had the idea of turning this scary experience into a research project, and Mikaila began to learn about bees and how they might become extinct in the future. Not long after, Mikaila decided to create a lemonade business, sweetening her lemonade with honey so it might be healthier and also help bees. She used her great-grandmother's lemonade recipe and created something new and innovative out of something old and cherished. Today, Mikaila is twelve years old and Me & the Bees Lemonade is sold in national grocery stores, including fifty-five locations of Whole Foods. Mikaila's business is thriving, and she donates a portion of all profits to charities benefiting honeybees and other natural causes. And she gets her homework done as she travels from place to place—including the White House!—to talk about her business.

I became fascinated with bees. I learned all about what they do for me and our ecosystem. So then I thought, what if I make something that helps honeybees and uses my Great Granny Helen's recipe?[5]

OLD WATER TO NEW WINE

*"The water that I will give will become in
them a spring of water gushing up to eternal life."*
John 4:14

Water. You can't live without it, but sometimes living with its storms and unpredictable floods can be devastating. On the sixth day of Creation God offered humanity dominion over the birds of the air and the fish of the sea, but God never offered dominion over the sea itself. God's spirit moved over the waters as if to remind them that they still must obey at least the wind. When we see water where it shouldn't be, our sensibilities urge us to build levees, dig channels, and fill sandbags; yet if we redirected the water entirely, we would live for just a few days.

Throughout Scripture, water offers a complex picture of God's world. It represents chaos, danger, and a barrier to the Promised Land, but it is never evil. Water is much more ambiguous than that, and as a result Jesus could assign it new meaning. One day Jesus sat with a Samaritan woman at a well and told her,

> *"Everyone who drinks of this water will be*
> *thirsty again, but those who drink of the water*
> *that I will give them will never be thirsty. The*
> *water that I will give will become in them a spring*
> *of water gushing up to eternal life."*
> *John 4:13-14*

Water takes the shape of the vessel in which it is carried. Film star and martial arts expert Bruce Lee once said,

> Be formless, shapeless, like water. Now, you put water into a cup, it becomes the cup. You put it into a teapot, it becomes the teapot. Now, water can flow, or creep, or drip—or crash. Be water, my friend.[6]

In the Gospels, water begins to take on new meaning. It becomes something through which we find rebirth. It is transformed into wine. It is something living that is offered to the outcast in Samaria. It flows from Jesus' side as he suffers on the cross. In his suffering, Jesus takes a symbol of chaos and transforms it into something life-giving, something that can wash away the dirt of life.

And yet, from the cross Jesus says, "I thirst." How can this be? How can the one who offers living water be thirsty?

Since Jesus' thirst is recorded only in John's poetic and theologically symbolic Gospel, perhaps something more is at work here. His thirst goes beyond sustenance. He thirsts for righteousness. He thirsts for justice with mercy. He thirsts for the kind of vessel in which living water would pool.

Diving even deeper into the story, wine plays a crucial role in the Gospels. Wine, it seems, is a symbol of a renewed creation. Jesus tells the Pharisees,

> *"No one puts new wine into old wineskins;*
> *otherwise the new wine will burst the skins and*
> *will be spilled, and the skins will be destroyed. But*
> *new wine must be put into fresh wineskins. And*
> *no one after drinking old wine desires new wine,*
> *but says, 'The old is good.'"*
>
> *Luke 5:37-39*

Luke in particular recognizes that the wine Jesus talks about is a picture of God's new creation in Christ. Luke, who wrote to those outside of the Jewish faith, emphasizes that being a follower of Jesus is a new way of living. In fact, Luke's is the only Gospel in which Jesus says at the Last Supper that the cup is the blood of a "new covenant" (Luke 22:20). Because Luke is written to outsiders, they were new to God's covenant of grace, mercy, and love. In other words, it's not that the covenant was new; rather, Luke's community was newly welcomed.

Jesus was someone who remembered God's story well. His life, suffering, death, and resurrection sparked a revolution that continues to change the world. Christ was in the beginning with God, older than time itself, but the covenant established on the cross and in the empty tomb offers us a new life rooted in mercy, forgiveness, grace, and love. As the old hymn reminds us, "Morning by morning, new mercies I see."[7]

There is old, there is new, and there is the covenant that fulfills them both.

What are some ways in which Jesus described or used water in his ministry?

John's Gospel is described as "poetic and theologically symbolic." In what ways is this true? What other adjectives would you use?

What does the word covenant *mean in the Christian faith? What does it mean to you personally?*

Chapter Six

LIFE, DEATH, AND RESURRECTION

When Superman comes face to face with Doomsday, a monstrous supervillain bent on death and destruction in Metropolis, the competition is fierce. The two fight each other to the death outside the offices of *The Daily Planet*. At the end of the story, Superman dies in the arms of Lois Lane.

The comic book storyline, called *The Death of Superman*,[1] gained all kinds of attention from national and international fans. Superman's death was shocking because the whole point of Superman is that he cannot be defeated. We want our heroes to struggle to keep the story interesting, but if Superman can be permanently defeated, is there any hope for "truth, justice, and the American way"? Superman is the leader of the Justice League and the archetype of what it means to be a superhero. If Superman is dead, then where does that leave us?

THE DEATH OF JESUS

It is finished.
John 19:30

In John 12, Jesus responds to the crowd, "The hour has come for the Son of Man to be glorified." I like to imagine that the crowd was roused into frenzy shouting, "Amen! Amen!" Jesus continues, "Very truly, I tell you, unless a grain of wheat falls into the earth and dies, it remains a single grain; but if it dies, it bears much fruit" (John 12:24). Now I imagine that the crowd responded with silent confusion. If Jesus dies, where does that leave us? What happens to the movement he started? Can Jesus even claim to be the Messiah if he is captured, beaten, and executed?

"To what shall I compare the kingdom of God?" Jesus asks (Luke 13:20). The Kingdom is like a mustard seed, a pearl, a treasure buried in a field. What do these images have in common? There may be several answers, but I think the point is that they are all planted or formed, buried into the earth or plunged into the depths of the sea. They are all born out of darkness. This is not exactly the image the crowd had in mind for their king; for Scripture says, "Although he had performed so many signs in their presence, they did not believe in him" (John 12:37).

When Jesus was nailed to the cross, Pilate added an inscription that read "Jesus of Nazareth, the King of the Jews." Many who saw this said, "Do not write, 'The King of Jews, but 'This man said, I am King of the Jews.'" "What I have written I have written," Pilate responded (John 19:19-22). The "Hosannas" ringing through the streets of Jerusalem quickly turned to denial and anger. The crowd would rather keep the mustard seed than allow it to be planted in hope. The crowd would rather protect the oyster than to irritate the system with a prophetic grain of sand. The crowd would rather defend the treasure than take the risk of burying it in a field.

Jesus is led away, carrying the cross to the outskirts of Jerusalem. He is nailed to the cross, and lifted up to be mocked while slowly and excruciatingly gasping for each breath. Jesus musters enough strength to say, "It is finished" (John 19:30). To the Roman authorities, this is welcome news. To those who shouted, "Crucify him," this sounds like permission to begin searching for a new zealot. To those who followed Jesus, this is a heart-breaking proclamation, because they now have to go home. It is finished. Jesus is dead. It is finished, but it isn't over.

The mustard seed is placed into the soil; the planting is finished, but growth has just begun. The grain of sand irritates the oyster and a pearl is formed; the pearl is finished, but it has not yet been strung together and admired as a work of art. The treasure has been buried; Christ is in the tomb, but the Kingdom is just beginning.

Superman has saved us time and time again, and if he really is dead, we might not make it to tomorrow. But Superman can sometimes be a crutch. I don't really have to love my neighbor with Superman flying around. If things get bad, Superman will just swoop in and fix them. There's not much reason to build up neighborhoods, improve education, feed the hungry, and clothe the naked. If it gets bad, Superman will know what to do.

Jesus isn't Superman. Jesus doesn't right the wrongs of the world through brute force and laser beams shooting from his eyes. Jesus showed us what it means to inherit the kingdom of God, a place where the poor are welcomed, the mourning are comforted, the religious authorities are held accountable, and in losing your life you find it. After showing us the Kingdom, Jesus breathed upon us the Holy Spirit, ascended into heaven, and told us that we are now his hands and feet in the world.

Jesus said from the cross, "It is finished," but the Kingdom was just beginning. It is finished . . . but it is not over. The mustard seed was planted, but the Kingdom's growth was just beginning.

What in our life needs to be "finished" so that we can enter into this Kingdom? During the season of Lent we "give things up," but what in our life really needs to be finished? Lent is not simply a time to give something up, knowing that come Easter Sunday we can pick it back up again. What do you need to put down never to pick up again? Maybe the drink that began as an easy way to unwind has become a crutch that you can't walk without? Maybe you began your career putting lots of hours in the office, for which you were rewarded, but now that work has become an anesthesia numbing your emotions to the stress that awaits you at home. Maybe you surround yourself with new clothes, a new phone, the club membership, hoping that something will fill the void that's killing you inside. It's not that these things shut the door of God's kingdom. The door is open. Salvation has been won. It's that they become barriers masking our sight, numbing our compassion, or becoming too large for us to climb or walk around. Jesus says, "It is finished," so let it be finished!

What do you think Jesus meant when he said, "It is finished"?

How does Superman become a crutch by fixing things again and again? How is Jesus different?

What in your life needs to be finished so you can enter the kingdom of God?

SUPERHEROES

Superman[2]

Comic

Publisher: DC Comics
Created by: Jerry Siegel and Joe Shuster
First appeared: *Action Comics* #1, May 1938.

Character

Alter Ego: Clark Kent
Species: Kryptonian
Home Planet: Krypton
Hometown: Smallville, Kansas
Currently resides in: Metropolis
Teams: Justice League

Powers

Super strength
Super speed
Super durability
Flight
Heat (laser) vision
Freezing breath

Enemies

Lex Luthor
Darkseid

Interesting fact

Superman is powerless over magic.

SUPERHEROES

Origin

Superman was born on the planet Krypton during the last days of its existence. His father is aware that their planet is dying and sends his newborn son, named Kal-El, away in a pod just before Krypton explodes. Kal-El's pod eventually lands in a field in the fictional Kansas town of Smallville. Kal-El is found by a farmer and his wife who decide to raise the strange alien boy as their own. They name him Clark.

As Clark grows up, he begins to develop his powers and has to learn how to use them. Clark moves to Metropolis where he works as a reporter, changing into his costume when the world needs Superman.

Heroic moment

When Superman sets out to end world hunger, he flies to impoverished places around the globe with a tanker filled with food. One dramatic stop gives a clue to Superman's motive and role model. As he heads toward Rio de Janeiro, he flies close to the iconic Christ the Redeemer statue that overlooks the city. With his arms outstretched, he mimics the statue's pose exactly. Even though he does not eliminate hunger, Superman still demonstrates the power of a life lived in imitation of Christ.[3]

SAVE US!

*Blessed is the king who comes in the name of
the Lord!*

Luke 19:38

The first song I ever downloaded on iTunes was "Save Me" by
Remy Zero. It was the theme song to *Smallville*, a television show
about a teenager who wrestles with his identity as a small-town kid
from Kansas, who just happens to be faster than a speeding bullet.
On my daily walk back and forth from seminary classes, I would
listen to the song on repeat and think about salvation. The chorus
goes, "Somebody save me . . . I don't care how you do it."[4]

About halfway through seminary, the song expressed how I
was feeling. How does Christ save us, and do the specifics matter?
Should we simply offer thanksgiving for a holy mystery we can't
comprehend? Are we supposed to understand the cross as payment
for the penalty of sin that only Christ could satisfy? Was Jesus born
to die, or was Good Friday a tragic, unintended consequence of
being obedient to God?

When Jesus entered into Jerusalem on the back of a donkey
during Passover week, the crowd shouted, "Hosanna!" meaning "Save us," and they had a very specific salvation in mind.
Depending on which Gospel you read, the crowd was either wav-
ing palms or spreading out their cloaks in recognition of Jesus as
king. Jesus' triumphal entry is a story heavy with tragic and pain-
ful irony. The crowd was shouting, "Blessed is the king," and the
Pharisees replied, "Teacher, order your disciples to stop." Jesus

answered, "I tell you, if these were silent, the stones would shout out" (Luke 19:39-40).

The crowd went on shouting, "Blessed is the king who comes in the name of the Lord" (Luke 19:38), but days later the same crowd was chanting, "Crucify him!" (Luke 23:21). The crowd quickly turned on Jesus, because he did not fit their definition of Messiah. Jesus did not deliver on the promises they thought he should have kept. They wanted Jesus to fit their own ideas. Jesus was supposed to be king, kick Rome out, and establish an earthly kingdom. Instead he got arrested, beaten, and mocked. So the crowd turned away, and if we are being honest, sometimes we do, too. Sometimes we get angry with God when our prayers are left unanswered, even if our prayers are selfish. We question whether God is there when our desires are unmet, even if those desires are misguided. We don't say, "Here I am Lord, send me." Instead, we say, "Come to me, Lord, because I like where I am."

The song "Bargain," by the Who, says, "I'm looking for that free ride to me, I'm looking for you." That's what the crowd was really shouting on that day when Jesus entered Jerusalem: "We are looking for the easy road to ourselves." But Jesus knows this about us and died for us anyway. Jesus knows and still chooses to love us.

Maybe we do cry for someone to save us, and maybe we don't care how they do it. The good news is that salvation is already here, and Christ offers us salvation through humility, generosity, obedience, and sacrifice. Salvation is not a quick road to ourselves; rather, we let go of ourselves so that we might learn to love God and love one another. As Paul puts it, "It is no longer I who live, but it is Christ who lives in me" (Galatians 2:20).

When you think of salvation, what do you envision? Do the details matter?

What does Jesus mean when he says, "If these were silent, the stones would shout out"?

What song lyrics speak to you about salvation, or offer insight into your relationship with God?

IN BETWEEN

This is my Son, my Chosen; listen to him!

Luke 9:35

The New Orleans Saints' victory in the 2009 Super Bowl, following Hurricane Katrina by just a few years, triggered a jubilant and desperately needed celebration across the city. Matthew Albright, opinion editor of Louisiana State University's *The Daily Reveille*, put it this way, "You can hear the bands marching down Canal Street. This isn't sophisticated, subtle music. . . . This is loud, proud, raw and wild like rolling thunder."[5]

It was the kind of celebration that breaks forth after years of suffering. It was Miriam on the shore of the Red Sea: "Sing to the Lord, for he has triumphed gloriously; / horse and rider he has thrown into the sea" (Exodus 15:21). It was David dancing before the ark of the covenant as it returned from Philistine exile. It was John the Baptist leaping in Elizabeth's womb at the sound of Mary's voice. It was Easter Sunday, when the tomb was empty and Mary ran to tell the disciples the news.

But what about the day before Easter? What about Saturday? The Saturday of Holy Week is like the valley between two great pillars, Good Friday and Easter Sunday. We don't know what to do with it. It's one of those in-between times.

Another in-between time is the season of Epiphany. The season begins dramatically with Jesus coming out of the waters hearing God's voice say, "You are my Son, the Beloved" (Luke 3:22). The season ends gloriously with Jesus descending the mountain, transfigured, again hearing God's voice say, "This is my Son, my Chosen; listen to him!" (Luke 9:35). But the in-between is so . . . in between.

Jesus goes up the mountain with Peter, James, and John to pray. While he is praying, the appearance of his face begins to change, and his clothes begin to shine. Then Jesus finds himself in between two pillars of the faith, Moses and Elijah, the Law and the Prophets. Jesus is in between the organized institution and the free-moving witness. But this is nothing new for Jesus. It's not that Jesus has one foot in divinity and one foot in humanity; he has both feet in divinity and both feet in humanity. He is the personification of in between.

Peter sees Jesus between the pillars of Moses and Elijah, and he wants to worship by building pillars for all three. Peter wants to remember this moment and all its glory, and who can blame him? Jesus, their guy, their rabbi, their Lord, is in the clouds speaking with Moses and Elijah. But Jesus comes down from the mountain and turns his face toward Jerusalem and the cross. From this moment on, everything will change.

Just a few short verses before, Jesus asked the disciples who they thought he was. Peter said, "You are the Messiah" and now Peter is beginning to realize what this means. Jesus begins speaking about his death. Peter doesn't want to hear it. He wants to build pillars.

He wants to worship this moment. He wants to remember the glory and the awe, and don't we? Why must we move down the mountain, Lord?

How do you observe Holy Saturday? Is it a day of mourning, expectation, or both?

How would you illustrate Epiphany and Transfiguration Sunday on a calendar?

What does it mean to say that Jesus has both feet in humanity and both feet in divinity?

REAL-LIFE HEROES

Chesley Sullenberger[6]

Chesley "Sully" Sullenberger is a former pilot for US Airways. In New York on January 15, 2009, the commuter plane he was flying was struck by a large flock of Canada geese. Both of the plane's engines were damaged, and Sullenberger made a fast decision to perform an emergency water landing in the Hudson River. He famously announced, "Brace for impact," as the plane came down on the water. The landing was a success, and all 155 people aboard the plane survived. Sullenberger was the very last person to leave the plane.

After he retired one year later, Sullenberger worked as a consultant on flight safety issues. His quick thinking and superior piloting skills meant life rather than death for everyone that day on what is now called the "Miracle on the Hudson."

We all have heard about ordinary people who find themselves in extraordinary situations. They act courageously or responsibly, and their efforts are described as if they opted to act that way on the spur of the moment. . . . I believe many people in those situations actually have made decisions years before. Somewhere along the line, they came to define the sort of person they wanted to be, and then they conducted their lives accordingly.[7]

WHEN EXPECTATION MEETS THE INCOMPREHENSIBLE

He is not here; for he has been raised, as he said.

Matthew 28:6

One Easter morning, a Sunday school teacher gave a kindergarten girl a bright, pastel-colored Easter egg. The little girl opened her egg and found a slip of paper with an Easter message. She struggled to sound out her newly found message. She read, "He is . . . a raisin?"

Of course, it makes no sense to say that Jesus is a raisin. But proclaiming that he is risen is simply incomprehensible. The Easter proclamation that Christ is risen stands in the tension between perception and reality, between form and content, between the way things are and the Way, the Truth, and the Life.

Easter is where expectation meets the incomprehensible. The women came to the tomb expecting the stillness and quiet of death, but in reality the earth shook, the stone rolled, and the heavens spoke: "He is not here; for he has been raised, as he said" (Matthew 28:6).

When expectation meets the incomprehensible, it leaves us with fear and great joy. Resurrection has changed everything. So, what does that mean? What does it mean for me, for us, for the church?

Easter means that death is no longer the end of your story. How much of my life is based on the assumption that death is the end?

When death is the end, then I hang on to my wealth and I try to have the biggest house and the fastest car. When death is the end, I can bury my secrets and faults and failures away so that when I die, they too will die.

Death is not the end of the story, which means there is redemption. Death is not the end of the story, which means there is forgiveness. Death is not the end of the story, which means your value is not based on what someone pays you. You are more than the stuff you fill your life with.

The women ran from the tomb in fear and great joy. Jesus had just walked out of the tomb, and what does that mean? It changes everything, and even good change brings with it some fear and trepidation. Jesus knows us so well. When he saw the women he said to them, "Do not be afraid."

Resurrection leaves us with fear and great joy. There is joy because Christ is alive and death has been defeated, but there is fear in the sense that what Jesus said is true. Turning the other cheek, giving our cloak, loving our enemies is what Jesus wants us to do and to reveal about God's kingdom. There is joy because there is life. There is fear because following Jesus means there is hard work ahead. Maybe this is why the resurrected Lord said, "Peace be with you. Do not be afraid."

So, what makes a hero? Resurrection does. Resurrection fills us with a fearlessness for the work that lies ahead. Resurrection fills us with the understanding that there is good, there is evil, and there is God who outshines the darkest of places with infinite goodness. Resurrection helps us understand that it's not about being right and resisting what is wrong, but that we are called out to be holy people, a holiness that defies categories. Resurrection isn't for us or them, but for all, so that together we might be the body of Christ, so that together we might be Christ's hands and feet in the world.

Resurrection reveals that the kingdom of God is a place where haves and have-nots understand the value of each other, and how that value is rooted in Christ, not in power or wealth or status. Resurrection reveals that the teachings of old can be trusted, and they can be experienced in a new way. Being made new is not something we put on a timeline, but through our connection with Christ we are made new every day.

Resurrection shows that our life is not about waiting for Superman to right our wrongs, but to get busy building God's kingdom. Resurrection reveals that death is not the end of the story. Resurrection teaches us that there is nothing to fear. Jesus said that his followers would do even greater works than he. Resurrection is what makes a hero. We are Resurrection people. Go and be a hero!

What does it mean to say that the Resurrection has changed everything?

According to this section, what is expectation, and what is incomprehensible? How do they meet?

In what ways is resurrection heroic? What does it mean for Jesus to be a hero?

Acknowledgments

I am so thankful to be able to share this study with you, but it would not have happened without some very special people. I first have to thank my wife, Christie, and my amazing children, Isabelle, Annaleigh, Cecilia, and Robert for sharing me with the ministry in general and this study in particular. I have to thank especially Asbury United Methodist Church in Bossier City, Louisiana, for offering me the grace to be always writing.

I must also lift up my colleagues in ministry who have helped me think through how our heroes inspire our faith, especially Rev. Dr. Sam Wells, Rev. Justin Coleman, Rev. Juan Huertas, Rev. John Robert Black, and Rev. Dr. Ken Evers-Hood. I also want to acknowledge the support of my colleagues in the Louisiana Conference of The United Methodist Church.

ACKNOWLEDGMENTS

I am so thankful to Abingdon Press for offering me this opportunity. To the team: Susan Salley, Ron Kidd, Alan Vermilye, Tim Cobb, Selena Cunningham, Marcia Myatt, Sonia Worsham, and Trey Ward. I also must lift up my editor, Maria Mayo, for all her hard work!

Notes

Introduction

1 Joseph Campbell, *The Hero with a Thousand Faces* (©Bollingen Foundation; published by Pantheon Books, 1949).

2 Christopher Vogler, "Hero's Journey," http://www.thewritersjourney .com/hero%27s_journey.htm. Accessed August 7, 2017.

Chapter One

1 "Batman," https://en.wikipedia.org/wiki/Batman. Accessed August 23, 2017.

2 *Detective Comics* (vol. 2, issue 1; DC Comics, 2011).

3 Desmond Tutu, *No Future Without Forgiveness* (New York: Doubleday, 1999), 158.

4 "Nelson Mandela," http://moralheroes.org/nelson-mandela. Accessed August 23, 2017.

5 Nelson Mandela, *Long Walk to Freedom: The Autobiography of Nelson Mandela* (New York: Back Bay Books, 1995), 622.

CHAPTER TWO

1   Les Daniels, *Marvel: Five Fabulous Decades of the World's Greatest Comics* (New York: Harry N. Abrams, 1991), 95.

2   "Spider-Man," https://en.wikipedia.org/wiki/Spider-Man. Accessed August 24, 2017.

3   *Spider-Man 3* (Columbia Pictures, 2007). https://www.youtube.com/watch?v=AM0eDg01rA8. Accessed August 24, 2017.

4   Rosa Parks and Jim Haskins, *Rosa Parks: My Story* (New York: Puffin Books, 1992), 116.

5   Julio Diaz on Story Corps, https://storycorps.org/listen/julio-diaz/. Accessed August 24, 2017.

6   "Harriet Tubman," http://www.history.com/topics/black-history/harriet-tubman. Accessed September 28, 2017.

7   Harriet Tubman, quoted in Sarah H. Bradford, *Scenes in the Life of Harriet Tubman* (1869).

CHAPTER THREE

1   CNN, "UN drops Wonder Woman as Honorary Ambassador," December 13, 2016, http://www.cnn.com/2016/12/13/health/wonder-woman-un-ambassador-trnd/index.html. Accessed August 24, 2017.

2   *Wonder Woman* (Warner Bros. Pictures, 2017). https://en.wikipedia.org/wiki/Wonder_Woman. Accessed August 27, 2017.

3   "Anne Frank," https://www.biography.com/people/anne-frank-9300892. Accessed August 24, 2017.

4   Anne Frank, *The Diary of a Young Girl* (New York: Alfred A. Knopf, 2010), 269.

CHAPTER FOUR

1   "Iron Man," https://en.wikipedia.org/wiki/Iron_Man. Accessed August 24, 1017.

2   Forbes, December 11, 2007, https://www.forbes.com/2007/12/11/tony-stark-money-oped-books-cx_de_fict1507_1211stark.html. Accessed August 25, 2017.

3   *The Invincible Iron Man* (#120–128; Marvel Comics, 1979).

4   Quoted in Jeff Kurtti, *Since the World Began: Walt Disney World: The First 25 Years* (New York: Disney Editions, 1996), 179.

5   *Coraline* (Laika, 2009).

6   "Saint Teresa of Calcutta," https://www.franciscanmedia.org /saint-teresa-of-calcutta/. Accessed August 26, 2017.

7   Statement of 1977, as quoted in Susan Ratcliffe, *Concise Oxford Dictionary of Quotations* (Oxford: Oxford University Press, 2011), 373.

8   Dr. Martin Luther King Jr., *Strength to Love* (Philadelphia: Fortress Press, 1981), 66.

CHAPTER FIVE

1   "Captain America," https://en.wikipedia.org/wiki/Captain _America. Accessed August 26, 2017.

2   *Captain America: The First Avenger* (Paramount Pictures, 2011). http://www.imdb.com/title/tt0458339/. Accessed August 26, 2017.

3   Michelle Nichols (12 July 2013). "Pakistan's Malala, Shot by Taliban, Takes Education Plea to U.N.". Reuters. Retrieved July 23, 2013.

4   "How This 11-Year-Old Turned Something Scary into Something Sweet," http://www.nbcnews.com/news/nbcblk/how-11-year-old -turned-something-scary-something-sweet-n545651. Accessed August 27, 2017.

5   "Me & the Bees Lemonade," https://meandthebees.com/pages /about-us. August 26, 2017.

6   John R. Little, *Bruce Lee: A Warrior's Journey* (New York: Contemporary Books, 2001), 59.

7   Thomas Chisholm, "Great Is Thy Faithfulness" (1923).

CHAPTER SIX

1   *The Death of Superman* (Superman, no. 75, Burbank, CA: DC Comics, 1993).

2   "Superman," https://en.wikipedia.org/wiki/Superman. Accessed August 27, 2017.

3   Paul Dini, *Superman: Peace on Earth* (Superman; DC Comics, 1998).

4   Remy Zero, *Save Me* (Santa Monica, CA: Geffen Records, 2001).

5   Matthew Albright, The Daily Reveille, http://www.lsunow.com /opinion/columnists/nietzche-is-dead-new-orleans-citizens -deserve-super-bowl-jubilation/. Accessed August 26, 2017.

6   "Chelsey Sullenberger," https://www.biography.com/people/chesley -sullenberger-20851353. Accessed September 28, 2017.

7   Chelsey B. Sullenberger III, *Highest Duty: My Search for What Really Matters* (New York: William Morrow, 2010), 184–185.